W9-ASG-520

CASE STUDIES IN

CULTURAL ANTHROPOLOGY

SERIES EDITORS

George and Louise Spindler

STANFORD UNIVERSITY

———————————

LIVES ON THE LINE
Women and Ecology on a Pacific Atoll

LIVES ON THE LINE
Women and Ecology on a Pacific Atoll

ALEXANDRA BREWIS

The University of Auckland

HARCOURT BRACE COLLEGE PUBLISHERS

Fort Worth   Philadelphia   San Diego   New York   Orlando   Austin   San Antonio
Toronto   Montreal   London   Sydney   Tokyo

Publisher	**Ted Buchholz**
Editor in Chief	**Christopher P. Klein**
Senior Acquisitions Editor	**Stephen T. Jordan**
Assistant Editor	**Linda Wiley/Margaret McAndrew Beasley**
Project Editor	**Pam Hatley**
Production Manager	**Lois West**
Art Director	**Sue Hart**

Cover Photo Three generations of Butaritari women

Copyright © 1996 by Harcourt Brace & Company

All rights reserved. No part of this publication may be reproduced or transmitted in any form or by any means, electronic or mechanical, including photocopy, recording, or any information storage and retrieval system, without permission in writing from the publisher.

Requests for permission to make copies of any part of the work should be mailed to: Permissions Department, Harcourt Brace & Company, 6277 Sea Harbor Drive, Orlando, Florida 32887-6777.

Address for Editorial Correspondence:
Harcourt Brace College Publishers
301 Commerce Street, Suite 3700
Fort Worth, TX 76102

Address for Orders:
Harcourt Brace & Company
6277 Sea Harbor Drive
Orlando, FL 32887-6777
1-800-782-4479, or 1-800-433-0001 (in Florida)

Printed in the United States of America

Library of Congress Catalog Card Number: 95-76341

ISBN 0-15-501969-4

5 6 7 8 9 0 1 2 3 4   066   10 9 8 7 6 5 4 3 2 1

Foreword

ABOUT THE SERIES

These case studies in cultural anthropology are designed for students in beginning and intermediate courses in the social sciences, to bring them insights into the richness and complexity of human life as it is lived in different ways, in different places. The authors are men and women who have lived in the societies they write about and who are professionally trained as observers and interpreters of human behavior. Also, the authors are teachers; in their writing, the needs of the student reader remain foremost. It is our belief that when an understanding of ways of life very different from one's own is gained, abstractions and generalizations about the human condition become meaningful.

The scope and character of the series has changed constantly since we published the first case studies in 1960, in keeping with our intention to represent anthropology as it is. We are concerned with the ways in which human groups and communities are coping with the massive changes wrought in their physical and sociopolitical environments in recent decades. We are also concerned with the ways in which established cultures have solved life's problems. And we want to include representation of the various modes of communication and emphasis that are being formed and re-formed as anthropology itself changes.

We think of this series as an instructional series, intended for use in the classroom. We, the editors, have always used case studies in our teaching, whether for beginning students or advanced graduate students. We start with case studies, whether from our own series or from elsewhere, and weave our way into theory, and then turn again to cases. For us, they are the grounding of our discipline.

ABOUT THE AUTHOR

Alexandra Brewis was born in Auckland, New Zealand, the eldest daughter of an engineer father and journalist mother. Brewis's first interest in the Pacific stems from her earliest childhood memories of growing up in a neighborhood of recent Pacific immigrants in Auckland in the 1960s, then and now the city with the largest Polynesian population.

Brewis moved to the Southwest desert in Tucson in 1988 and in 1992 completed a Ph.D. in anthropology at the University of Arizona. She returned home to take up a position in the Department of Anthropology at The University of Auckland, where she teaches undergraduate and graduate classes in human biology, medical anthropology, human evolution, and gender.

Following her research in Kiribati in 1990 and 1991, Brewis has published a number of articles dealing with fertility and sexuality in the Pacific. Her ongoing interest in the ecology of reproduction in small island populations continues in her current research, which most recently has concentrated on developing new projects on fertility and family planning in Western Samoa and a study of anti-fertility plant use in the region.

ABOUT THIS CASE STUDY

This is the only case study in our series about a people and their culture resident on a land mass only about fifteen kilometers long and a few hundred meters wide surrounded by a limitless expanse of ocean. It is notable, not only for this compelling circumstance, but because it is a study of women's lifeways within this context.

The author, a young unmarried woman, came to know the details of life in the family and of the lives of women within it, as well as their movements and involvements in social space outside the family and in the complex of relationships between family and community. No aspect of women's lives escapes scrutiny. Subsistence and economics, power and politics, childbearing and child rearing and women's health, relationships among women and between women and men, and sexual behavior in social and physical contexts are illuminated by descriptive analyses that could be written only by someone who had lived through the situations and the complex relationships of Butaritari life as experienced and perceived by women.

Dr. Brewis walked a tightrope to attain this intimacy. As a single, unmarried, and attractive young woman, she ran a constant risk of eliciting too much attention from males; associating too closely with *nikiranroro*—most inclusively, socially labeled unmarried nonvirgins; and alienating the respectable married or soon-to-be-married women. She negotiated this tightrope with good judgment and civil skill. The result is this intimately detailed, well-balanced case study.

The writing in this case study is characterized by a reflexive style that brings the reader to the people of Butaritari through direct personal experience and observation. She does not sacrifice or endanger careful attention to data that leads to both understanding Butaritari behavior with some degree of empathy and understanding it as related to ecology and women's adaptations to the realities of life on a minuscule atoll.

It is to the author's credit that she puts Butaritari in perspective as not a world in itself. Though separated from other inhabited places by miles of open sea and out of the lanes of world traffic, Butaritari has a place in the world history and in the sociopolitical developments of the twentieth century. Dr. Brewis attends to these relationships as the text unfolds. This case study is worthy of serious attention by colleagues and students alike.

George and Louise Spindler
Series Editors
Ethnographics
P.O. Box 38
Calistoga, CA 94515

ACKNOWLEDGMENTS

I am deeply indebted to all those who have provided emotional, intellectual, and financial support in undertaking and writing about this research. For their assistance in Kiribati, I would like to particularly thank Nei Kaneakia and the family of Neboata and Tonganibeia, Nei Taonatari, Bwere Eritaia, Doctor Tetaua Taitai, Nei Mareve, Roreti Tetao, Nei Toka Corbett, Shane Pike, John Vanderwee, Kevin Walters, and the staff of the Kiribati National Archives and Tungaru Central Hospital Medical Statistics Unit.

I am most grateful to my anthropological colleagues at the University of Auckland, especially Judith Huntsman, Douglas Sutton, Thegn Ladefoged, and John Allen, for providing such a congenial environment in which to think, argue, and write about the Pacific. Joan Lawrence provided the illustrations, and Hamish MacDonald prepared the photographs. Further afield, I am very grateful to Jane Underwood, Andrea Wiley, Bernd Lambert, and Steven T. McGarvey for their insights. I am thankful for the mentoral support for this research project I received from faculty at the University of Arizona's Department of Anthropology. I also offer a very special and personal thank you to Louise Senior and Dunbar Bernie for their friendship in Tucson and at longer distances.

Financial support was provided by the Health Research Council of New Zealand and the Population Science Division of the Rockefeller Foundation. An Andrew W. Mellon Foundation Fellowship in 1992–1994, held in the Population Studies and Training Center at Brown University, provided the time and intellectual environment in which to conceive this particular treatment of Butaritari data. A grant from the University of Auckland Research Committee supported the completion of this text.

This book is in essence a distillation of the trust and friendship given to me by the women of Butaritari—women of dignity and grace. I owe them the greatest debt of gratitude for their hospitality, protection, and kindness. I only pray I live up to the gift of their trust.

Alexandra Brewis
Auckland, New Zealand

A Note on Terminology

Two particularly unexpected pronunciations of Northern Kiribati words follow:

ti   pronounced as *si* (see)
tu   pronounced as *su* (soo)

Kiribati is pronounced Ki-ri-bas. Spellings of Kiribati words follow Sabatier's dictionary, except where regional usage varies.

Te is the basic article, equivalent to *a, an,* and *the* in English.
Nei is the general article before women's names, like "Ms." in English.

For simplicity's sake, I have used the term the Butaritari to refer to the people of Butaritari Atoll. The atolls that comprise the Republic of Kiribati were previously part of the Gilbert and Ellice Islands Colony, renamed Kiribati at independence. The islands of Tungaru, the local name, were previously called the Gilbert chain of the colony.

All names in the text with an asterisk (*) are pseudonyms. All others are those of the people concerned.

Contents

Illustrations

For Jane.
Thank you.

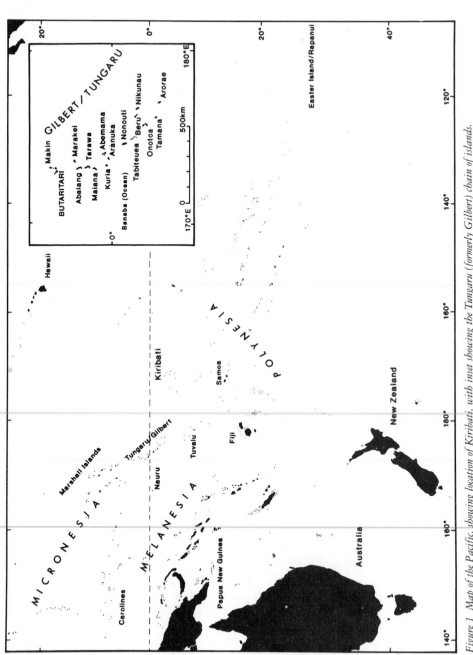

The inset map labels:

GILBERT/TUNGARU

BUTARITARI
Makin
Abaiang — Marakei
Maiana — Tarawa
Kuria — Abemama
Aranuka
Banaba (Ocean) — Nonouti
Tabiteuea — Beru — Nikunau
Onotoa
Tamana — Arorae

170°E   0   500km   180°E

Main map labels:

MICRONESIA
Carolines
Marshall Islands
Hawaii
Tungaru/Gilbert
Nauru
Kiribati
Tuvalu
Fiji
Samoa
MELANESIA
Papua New Guinea
Australia
New Zealand
POLYNESIA
Easter Island/Rapanui

140°   160°   180°   160°   140°   120°   40°

20°   0°   20°   40°

Figure 1   Map of the Pacific, showing location of Kiribati, with inset showing the Tungaru (formerly Gilbert) chain of islands.

Introduction

Between mid-1990 and 1991 I spent a year doing anthropological research and living as a young, single woman on the isolated central Pacific island of Butaritari. Interested in the environmental context of human reproduction, I had chosen Butaritari as a research site in part because of its geographic finiteness and the relative isolation of the people living there. I hoped that in the stark and circumscribed setting of a rural atoll the complex connections between human fertility, biology, and behavior and the broader environment would be especially evident.

My impression on my first sighting of the island, from the window of a small Trilander plane, reassured me this would be the case. At first only a thin smudge of green could be picked out on the horizon. As the plane drew closer, it expanded into a ribbon of land traced with a frill of white beach and foaming waves. As the plane banked toward the landing strip, the lagoon spread light and blue in our path, reaching out to the distant, red edge of the reef. The reef started to take shape, and I could make out human forms swimming along and standing on the reef edge. Each human shape was traced with a wide, dark shadow, the menacing and omnipresent forms of tiger sharks trailing fisherfolk. As we made a final approach to a runway cut from the thin strip of land between reef and lagoon, the green ribbon expanded into thick stands of coconut trees. I could pick out thatched roofs between the trees, organized neatly along the edge of a narrow, white coral road.

I still recall vividly this first startling visual image of Butaritari Atoll—of dazzling light, bright colors, and sharp lines. But most forcefully, I was struck by the absolute lack of land and the sense of the intrusion of the sea. A letter written later that same evening to a friend in the United States reminds me that the emotional impression of that sense of finiteness was just as strong as the visual one:

> It's _very_ small. I can't imagine how I'll last here for a year without going completely mad. I read somewhere that the U.S. commander on Johnson Atoll went island crazy and tried to drive his jeep to America. He ended up, vehicle and all, sinking into the lagoon. They shipped him home in a straight jacket. This place is much smaller than Johnson! It takes about twenty seconds to walk from one coast to the other. There's no escape from the sea—it can be heard, smelt and seen from anywhere on the island. My only saving grace may be that I don't have a jeep, only a bicycle.

Geographically speaking, probably no other places on the globe manifest the sense and reality of isolation and smallness as keenly as on a Pacific atoll. Butaritari, some fifteen kilometers long and a mere few hundred meters wide, sits at the very north of the Tungaru (or Gilbert) chain of islands. It is typical of atolls in the Pacific

Butaritari island looking northeast from the air. On the right is the reef edge, to the left the lagoon.

Ocean: It is breathtakingly beautiful but also flat, small, isolated, and resource-poor. These harsh realities of atoll geography permeate all aspects of the lives of those who live on them—you cannot avoid the practical boundaries of human activity when you live on a tiny lump of coral in the middle of the world's largest ocean.

Although remote and having very little land, Pacific atolls hardly can be described as self-contained universes. The islands of Tungaru sit on the "line" or equator at the interface of the geographic and cultural regions of Micronesia and Polynesia and have long-term ties to both. Before European incursion into the region, Pacific islanders were skilled sailors and navigators and traveled extensively to explore, settle, trade, and marry (Irwin 1992). Butaritari oral history recounts epic voyages southeast to Polynesia and northwest into Micronesia over the last several centuries and traces genealogical connections between the aristocracy of Butaritari and those of Samoa and the Marshall Islands.

According to radiocarbon dates estimated from skeletons excavated by a team of Japanese archaeologists on Makin, the island was settled sometime before A.D. 400. The initial settlers were likely to have come from the north in the region of the Marshall or Caroline groups. This inference is based on two lines of evidence: linguistic and genetic. The language spoken in the chain is closely related to those in Eastern Micronesia, such as the Marshalls and Carolines, although it also contains many words borrowed from Polynesia to the south.

In molecular genetics, the sequences of codes on human DNA in different groups are examined to show the amount of similarity. The more similar the sequences, the closer the populations are thought to be; that is, the more recently they shared the same gene pool. On the basis of the few samples tested from Kiribati, DNA sequences appear most similar to those of groups to the north and west in Micronesia, rather than south and east in Polynensia. Micronesia as a whole has emerged looking somewhat like a genetic mixed bag, though, showing clear but very complex affinities to Southeast Asian gene pools as well as to those in Melanesia to the south. Until this complexity can be addressed through improved sampling, the ultimate origins of Micronesians, including *I Kiribati* (the people of Kiribati), are yet to be settled.

More recent history records hundreds of purposeful and accidental voyages beyond the Gilbert chain, some as far as Papua New Guinea and the western edge of Micronesia, as well as marriages by both men and women to people from other Pacific islands. Today, life on the atolls of Kiribati is linked economically and politically to broader national and global processes; people find a need for cash to purchase imported tea, sugar, and matches and leave the island to earn income on the phosphate island of Nauru or as seamen on German ships. Global changes in copra prices change the way people farm coconut, and introduced diseases kill children.

This book is about how the constraints of ecology and the contingencies of history weave through patterns of human activity on Butaritari Atoll, using examples in the arena of women's health, sexuality, and fertility. In an ecological approach, the researcher focuses on studying the relationship between humans and the environment in which they attempt to live and reproduce. Human behavior, and the immediate sociocultural and biological contexts in which it takes place and from which it emerges, cannot be considered as unconnected to broader issues of the environment. The environment in this sense includes all animal and plant life and all physical elements, such as water, temperature, and terrain, as well as the environment of social interactions and institutions. Specifically, the starting point of an ecological approach is the assumption that we are all inescapably actors in an "ecological theater"—that to understand our behavioral repertoires we need to understand the environment in which they play out. We expect, for example, to see behavioral differences among Arctic Inuit, Australian desert dwellers, and high-altitude Tibetan farmers who are linked, directly or indirectly, to the extremes of the environments in which they live. Where Inuit are more concerned socially, technologically, and biologically with the necessities of warmth and shelter, desert dwellers are more focused on the role of water and water conservation. In the same vein, in the small island setting of Butaritari, land and land-hunger are examples of central themes in social interaction and patterning.

This case study is also about the lives of the women I met and came to know on Butaritari, and these women emerge as the principal actors in this text. A focus on their concerns, thoughts, and lives evolved out of the research topic and the practicalities of doing fieldwork in the arena of fertility studies, rather than as an explicit decision on my part to spotlight women in the research process. In Butaritari society, as in many other places, reproduction and parenting are considered to be predominantly women's concerns. Butaritari women have more direct experience and more esoteric knowledge of the topics I was investigating and were also more likely to wish to spend time talking about them.

Generally, anthropologists need to learn more about women's lives. Over the last two decades, the development of a feminist anthropology has made it clear that the potential of women's contribution to our understanding of human social life and history has been often ignored or underexplored in anthropological writings. Most ethnography has been written from and interpreted through male perspectives— whether as researchers or as informants or, more often, as both. And the topics that more often centrally concern women have been dismissed historically as less important or illuminating domains of human experience. We need to more actively study women's lives because they have as much to offer to our understanding of human experience as studies of activities, such as warfare or ritual, more usually associated with men. A significant advantage of such a gendered perspective as the one used in this book is that it begins with the position that those topics specifically concerning women, like motherhood, and those events in which women are the central actors, like birth, are valuable to research in their own right.

If this text is about women on Butaritari, it also is an outcome of the personal experience I had as a young woman doing field-based research on human reproduction. At the level of basic description, my fieldwork used the same techniques as most anthropological research: doing census surveys, taking life histories, asking formal questions in interviews and informal questions as opportunities arose in day-to-day interaction, spending time learning from specialists—in my case, eight local healers—and collating and copying archival materials. Doing fieldwork in rural and nonindustrial settings, a long way from power points or regular supplies, is an often frustrating and messily impractical business, in which everything that can go wrong usually does. My field experience in Butaritari was also very typical in this regard: Important notes were lost off the side of a boat in the middle of the lagoon, my computer drowned in a heavy rainstorm, and a rat feasted on my most valued food supplies. And fieldwork is always an intense and individual experience, and each field situation poses its own special challenges to both the anthropologist and locals as they attempt to live and work together. In my case, sexuality became the touchstone.

Butaritari island is connected by regular flights to the administrative capital of Tarawa. The arrival of each plane causes excitement, especially for children.

The author taking field notes during an interview, in standard village dress and hairstyle.

Being a single *I Matang* (Western) woman studying sexuality in a society where single women are generally more reticent and innocent than I appeared to be provided a host of emotional and practical contradictions—not only to my hosts, but also to me. The issue of the relationship between my own sexuality and the nature of my research was placed front and center.

Even despite a recent flourishing of more autobiographical or "reflexive" writing by anthropologists—which acknowledges and discusses how personal identity, including whether partnered or single, male or female, and so on, impacts the research experience and its interpretation—the issues of field-worker sexuality and sexual identity are rarely grappled with, at least openly. One seasoned woman anthropologist recently noted that the problem of sexuality and sexual risk for ethnographers:

> . . . is an area of vulnerability not merely in the physical sense, but in the sense that in the field we are even less free than elsewhere to construct our own sexuality—it is largely constructed for us and sometimes in spite of us (Caplan 1993:23–24).

It is also notable that, when field workers do discuss sex, the issues appear different for men and women: Men talk more of mutual attractions and women of sexual threat and perceptions of risk (Wade 1993; Warren 1988). If this is the case, my emotional experiences as a single woman in the field are hardly unique. Perhaps, though, adding my attempts to study sexual behavior heightened the issue in both practical and emotional terms. I was forced to develop a workable "sexual persona"—a balance between projecting enough sexual experience to be able to speak openly with women about sex but maintaining enough sexual reticence to feel sufficiently safe from sexual threat as I perceived it.

Sexual coercion of women by men is a common theme in Butaritari society, and sexual violence against women is not rare. I felt physically threatened on many occasions, and in many ways this shaped my ability to conduct research and travel about on the one hand, but drew me further into the women's community on the other. Spending time discussing these issues probably made them more real and personally threatening than they may otherwise have been. Listening to women's narratives of sexual coercion certainly threw the issue into sharp relief.

The personal threat of sexual coercion was greatly complicated by the nature of my research and was often difficult to balance. It is inappropriate for young Butaritari women of "good character" to travel alone between villages or to sleep away from the protection of relatives. To do otherwise, women run the risk of being perceived as sexually accessible. This reality of life on the atoll had immediate practical ramifications. I could not live alone without taking significant precautions (although little more than the comparable precautions I take in large American cities). My female friends told me stories about what could happen to women in the bush alone and, as they intended, scared me out of moving around outside the village by myself. This made it difficult to work outside of Butaritari village, where I was living. It also meant I had very little "time-out" on my own, which I often felt I needed living in a busy village full of open-sided huts and a constant flow of visitors to my household. It was difficult to retreat with any sense of safety to the more deserted tracts of the island and have any private time.

It also was extremely difficult to have any conversation about sexuality with a man without it being misconstrued. Although I avoided specific social contact with men and showed no demonstrable interest in village men, married or not, only married or sexually experienced women can discuss sexual matters. The language of sex is denied to young, unmarried women—and I was not married. This created difficulties

Nei Kaneakia, on the right, was my valued field assistant for much of the time I was on Butaritari. She and I have been interviewing an unaine *(old woman) in her home about the births of her thirteen children.*

because I was attempting to avoid being seen as a specifically sexual being, to avoid what I perceived as the threat of sexual coercion, but I was trying to discuss sex often as part of my research program. The tightrope I walked was trying to create a balance between my sexual reputation, personal safety, and my research interests. I was generally successful at managing to negotiate these, but it was always tricky, and ultimately it kept me from ever feeling a "true participant" in daily village activity.

One research limitation of essentially keeping away from men is I have only an indirect understanding of any male perspective of Butaritari sexuality or parenting. I was reliant on Butaritari women to present the views of their husbands, fathers, sons, and brothers, and the material about men comes with this clear proviso.

If sex is a problematic personal issue for field researchers, we also lack any sophisticated understanding of human sexuality within the broadly theoretical frameworks of anthropology. We know very little, for example, about how sexuality and sexual behavior vary within and between different human groups. If part of our understanding stems from the difficulties—practical and emotional—of studying sex, our discipline also has historically failed to develop, or even attempt to develop, a systematic analytical understanding of human sexual behavior. This is despite an early and vigorous interest in human sexuality linked to the modern roots of anthropology. One "father" of anthropology, Branislaw Malinowski, had much to say on the subject in his analyses of the functional nature of human societies. Maybe even too much, he noted, admitting in 1932, "I alone have to plead guilty to four books on the subject, two of which have the word sex on the title-page" (cited in Tuzin 1991). Despite this early precedent, by the early 1980s anthropologists had, in the interim decades, produced little more than a fascinating mountain of erotica or "ethnopornography" (Pellow 1990). In part this is the result of some provincial views toward sex within our discipline and broader Western society. In many ways, as Western researchers we have been culture-bound, constrained in our ability to study patterns of sexual behavior by our own cultural taboos that define sex as an intimate, "deviant" sphere of human life.

A dearth of solid cross-cultural studies has made it difficult for anthropology as a discipline to deal with the demands of such growing contemporary issues as sexually transmitted disease, teenage motherhood, or sexual violence, because we simply do not have enough quality basic research on which to draw. This situation is changing, though, with anthropological research into human sexual behavior becoming more legitimized and sophisticated as it becomes more topical and also better funded. If one phenomenon can be pointed to as significant in this regard, it is the publicizing of the AIDS epidemic, which has demystified and de-tabooed many aspects of sexual activity, or at least of the study of sexual activity, in such countries as the United States.

Even so, much of the proliferation of research on sexuality in anthropology in the last decade has focused on the symbolic construction of sexual meanings. While this has enhanced our understanding of the dynamics of gender relations, we have very few descriptions of the actual nature of sexual acts and the immediate contexts —emotional, social, economic, cultural, and biological—in which it takes place, particularly from the cross-cultural perspective. Rather, we have a growing stack of texts that discuss sexuality but seemingly negate the idea that sexuality has anything to do with actually having sex. Instead:

... the erotic dissolves in questions of rank, and images of male and female bodies, sexual substances, and reproductive acts are peeled back to reveal an abiding concern for military honors, the pig herd, and the estate (Ortner and Whitehead 1981:24).

In discussing sexual activity in this book, one of my aims is to make explicit an ethnography of sexual behavior, in part to address a relative lack of such studies. And, if anthropology is short on basic grounded descriptions of human sexual activity, even more rare are analyses that focus on women's sex and sexuality rather than men's.

Studies of sex have not only been constrained by their vaguely dubious historical status within anthropology but also by the complicated practicalities that emerge in any investigation of particularly private human activities. It is a virtual universal that sexual acts are shrouded in intimacy. Sex is especially difficult to study, in that the cultural prescriptions for appropriate sexual activity are often highly inaccurate indices of what people do once others are not watching. Studies of sexual activity cannot readily rely on the ethnographic bread-and-butter method of participant observation, instead having to rest on people's self-reports of their activities—a situation where normative responses are more likely to emerge at the expense of the researcher being able to elicit "reliable" answers from people about their sex lives. That is, a chasmic gap often occurs between ideology and experience, between what people say they do and what they actually do.

Advantageously, in the case of Butaritari, people are quite comfortable discussing sex. Butaritari women talk, joke, and gossip about sex, sex acts, and organs as part of day-to-day discourse. It does not strike them as particularly strange—

Early in the field season these women assisted in taking a census of everyone living on the island.

although somewhat amusing—that I might be interested in the subject and want to talk with them a lot about it. Interviews were very open, informal affairs, and, over the course of my year on Butaritari, sex was not only discussed and debated at great length in interviews but also initiated by the women in many informal interactions, such as lying about at my house drinking tea and lazily gossiping in the heat of the early afternoon. All in all, I feel confident that what I write here about sex in Butaritari reflects the experience of sexual behavior, inasmuch as I believe the women were trying to give me essentially "honest" answers. The whole issue of ethnographic validity and sexual activity is obviously thorny, but my relationships with the women with whom I worked were warm and open. The women were very interested in and supportive of my research. I feel incredibly fortunate to have been taken into their confidence, and I hope the text that follows lives up to that trust.

1 / Contact and Isolation: Butaritari Ecology and History

In the beginning when earth and the sky were still sealed together there was only the giant spider Nareau. He cleft the earth and the sky and then walked out across the ocean. In those places where his feet touched the sea, islands welled up. And so, the islands of Tungaru are the footprints of Nareau.

Kiribati creation story

Butaritari is an atoll or coral-reef island. It began with colonies of lime-secreting polyps living in the warm, shallow water above a submerged volcanic cone. As the tiny creatures died, the colony continued to build on their skeletons, slowly rising toward the ocean surface. Eventually, a narrow land mass emerged, reaching only a few meters above sea level.

Atolls can form a perfect ring of land enclosing a lagoon, mimicking as they do the form of the volcanic cone below (see Figure 2). On Butaritari the form is less uniform, and the roughly circular land mass is broken into fragments separated by stretches of water running between the reef on one side and the lagoon on the other. The wide channel between Keuea and Tanimainiku has been breached with a coral-rock causeway. Until this was built, journeys to the northeastern end of the island had to wait until low tide. To get to the farthermost edge of the reef and the isolated village on Bikati islet still requires a boat.

True to the desert-island image, Butaritari has no natural sources of water, except for rainfall. Although the sea invades the porous rock under the island, rainwater seeps quickly through the soil and is trapped in a lens on top of the salt water. The water is then reclaimed from wells dug through the soft rock. The water level in the wells drops and rises with each rainfall and each turning of the tide.

Although proportionately more rain falls between February and April, it rains all year round on an almost daily basis. The rains are sudden, heavy, and loud. So close to the equator no real seasons, no change in the length of days, and no notable changes in temperature occur. Robert Louis Stevenson, the Scottish writer of such tropical tales as *Treasure Island,* stayed on Butaritari for several months in 1899 and painted a romantic and deserved portrait of the Butaritari climate, saying it enjoys "a superb ocean climate, days of blinding sun and bracing winds, nights of heavenly brightness" (1987:224). My only reservation would be over the romance of constant heat, being a very humid and invariant 28 degrees Celsius (82.4 degrees Fahrenheit). In the first month I was on Butaritari, I battled constant exhaustion in the afternoon heat and a series of uncomfortable and embarrassing heat rashes. However, once I learned to sleep long and often and anywhere, and always in the early afternoon, as is the style in Butaritari, these problems disappeared.

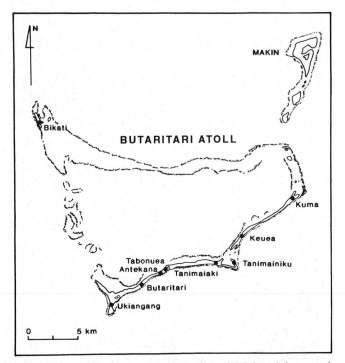

*Figure 2   Map of Butaritari Atoll, showing Butaritari village (labeled) and the seven other main vil-
lages. Butaritari village is the largest village, with more than a quarter of the islands' population. Many
Butaritari have relatives on the satellite island of Makin and regular contact occurs between the two
islands. With favorable tide and current, the trip between the two is bumpy but short.*

Flat atoll geography offers little protection from high seas. Tropical typhoons
cause massive destruction to small islands, and typhoons in the small atolls of Polynesia and Micronesia are dramatic and frightening to those who live through them.
Waves may rise up to thirty feet above the beach, and land is transformed into ocean.
Coconut palms are toppled, crops mauled, and houses shredded. Butaritari is situated
in a climatically quiet zone that straddles the equator and keeps the island out of the
path of many typhoon winds and tropical cyclones. This does not mean the island is
exempt. In 1928 a powerful hurricane stormed across the island, damaging thou-
sands of coconut trees and houses—although luckily at no cost to lives.

The Butaritari depict the lagoon side of the island as feminine and tame. The lagoon beach runs down from the road to the water in a graceful sweep of white sand
(see Figures 3 and 4). On the other edge of the island is the reef and the open
ocean—the male, aggressive side of the island—where the drop-off to the sea is
more precipitous. A flat block of coral debris runs along the ocean side, usually
empty of both plants and animals, separating land and ocean and providing a break
to the crash of waves at high tide. The eight main villages on the island are spread
along the lagoon edge, each separated from the next by lonely stretches of thick coconut forest and scrub bush that spill into unplanted swamps filled with small fish
and wild taro, a coarse root crop. In each village the houses are spread out along the

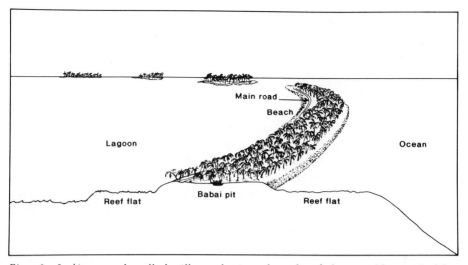

Figure 3   Looking across the atoll, the village and main road run along the less-exposed lagoon side of the island, and the gardens extend toward the reef.

wide coral road, spaced between breadfruit trees, orange-fruited pandanus, and co-conut palms.

Houses are built of mainly local materials, such as breadfruit wood and pan-danus roots, tied together with coconut-husk fiber, and thatched with prickly, dried pandanus leaves. Built open-sided to let the breeze through, they can be screened with woven coconut leaves for privacy and filled with pandanus-leaf mats for com-fort. People sleep on covered platforms, stretched out on mats and shrouded in mos-quito nets.

Each household has one or more of these open-sided huts, a screened washing area, and a cooking hut. The area between the huts is covered with a thick floor of broken, weathered, white pieces of coral and shell carted from the reef front. It keeps the area tidy and clean but is sharp on the feet and harshly bright on the eyes. The household plot, or *kainga,* usually stretches from lagoon to reef, taking in taro

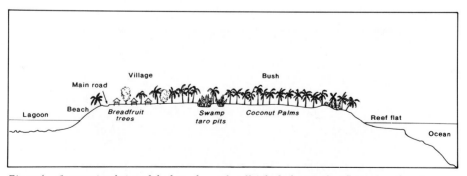

Figure 4   Cross-sectional view of the form of a coral atoll. The fresh-water lens floats above the salt water under the atoll surface.

gardens, toddy palms, and breadfruit, which can be harvested when it is inconvenient to walk to the bush to the larger land plots.

FOOD SOURCES AND ECONOMIC ACTIVITY

The coral atoll, with such small land area, so reliant on rain water, and so flat and exposed to the elements, is one of the most resource-limited land forms. On Butaritari, the constant downpours and even temperatures keep the island comparatively lush and assist in breaking down the coral base rock into soil. Yet the actual number of plant and animal species that can flourish on an atoll, however verdant, are relatively few. Having spent enormous energy trying to grow several crops in a kitchen garden—watermelon and tomato included—I learned the reality of farming on an atoll. Many plants simply cannot tolerate the challenge of sandy, alkaline soil. Lacking any mineral deposits—except bird droppings—atoll soils require constant replenishment with organic material before even hardy crops can survive.

Although the range of land-based resources may be limited, seafood is plentiful. Fish are caught from still canoes in the lagoon, from trolls in open ocean, by spear off the reef, or from lines on the shore. At full moon, torches can be seen flashing on the water from beyond the reef, marking those fishing by scoop-netting for flying fish. From the reef come octopus and lobster; from the beach come shellfish and the long, skinny sandworms that are gutted and dried and chewed as a sort of worm jerky. For special occasions, enormous, green sea turtles are captured. They are kept

A view of abandoned swampland between Ukiangang and Butaritari village.

fresh for several days by being tipped upside down on their backs so they stay alive but cannot escape. Baked with the skin on, sea turtle has a tangy, salty taste. Another special-occasion food is the rich, oily flesh of the giant clam *(Tridacna)* harvested from the reef.

The one fish sold locally is tuna, which is also shipped to the administrative center of Tarawa, one of the Tungaru islands, to provide extra cash for local fishers. Myriad types of lagoon, reef, and open-sea fish are eaten fried, barbecued, and cooked in the earth. Fillets are also preserved by salting and sun-drying.

Coconut, pandanus, breadfruit, and giant swamp taro are the important everyday foods. Coconuts grow everywhere, being very tolerant of salt and salty water, and can grow well in even the poor, chalky soils. The coconut at different stages produces a wide range of foods. Young green nuts contain a refreshing, ready drink of juice, and the young, jellylike flesh makes an excellent soft food for young children. As the coconut matures, the white flesh becomes oilier and harder. The flesh is grated as a flavor for drinks and food and squeezed into coconut cream. Dried in the sun, the flesh can be boiled down to a fragrant oil for cooking, healing, and grooming. Left to germinate, the center of the nut grows an edible, thick, crunchy flesh that is eaten raw or cooked into a spongy mush. The husks are burnt as fuel in the kitchen fire, or the fibers are stripped and rolled to make rope, and the shells that encase the flesh are scraped clean to use as containers or burned down into charcoal.

The coconut palm is particularly valued for its toddy, the sugary sap of the coconut palm flower spathe that is drunk both fresh and fermented and boiled down

Here coconuts lie drying in the sun, in preparation to be sold as copra. The house in the background is typical on Butaritari, open-sided, with a wooden platform and pandanus-leaf thatch on the roof.

to be preserved as a molasses-style candy or syrup. Toddy is vitamin-rich, especially in B and C, and very sweet—some 540 kcal/liter or 16 percent sugar. In the southern islands of the chain, it has been credited with keeping people not only alive but also corpulent even during prolonged droughts.

Second to the coconut as a staple is the pandanus, a large, attractive, spiky plant related to the pineapple, for which the Butaritari have some 160 different names. Under the sharp, long, thorny leaves, long, hard roots trace their way to the ground from several feet up the trunk, forming a thick, straight fan. The plants are dispersed through the bush, either alone or in thick, prickly stands. The large clusters of fruit ripen from green to orange—into the colors of sexual tumescence, according to Butaritari descriptions:

> *It was Te Raka from Butaritari who taught the Nauruans how to eat pandanus after he flew to Nauru by covering himself with the feathers of a giant bird. When the pandanus ripen in a bunch, they glow red and open. The Nauruans were scared to eat them and ran away from the fruits because they thought they were women's genitalia. Te Raka laughed at the Nauruans and told them they were not a woman's thing. He bit into the fruit and encouraged them to do the same. This is how the Nauruans learned to enjoy the pandanus.*
> Butaritari legend

The fruit are eaten fresh as a stringy, crunchy snack. I find raw pandanus a little tasteless but delicious when baked into a cake with coconut to liven the flavor. Pandanus was more prolific on the atoll before the growth of the copra trade, at which stage coconut became the propagate of choice.

Breadfruit, also called jackfruit, is one of the few seasonal crops. It grows near houses and along the side of the road, producing a large, ovular, dimpled, green fruit between May and December. Hanging high from the ground in tall, arching trees, the fruit are knocked to the ground with a knife attached to a long pole. During high winds the fruit come flying off the tree and boom onto roads and roofs. I know of at least one case where this proved lethal: A young boy was killed when a flying breadfruit hit him on the bridge of his nose. The fruit has a delicate flavor when eaten raw and is served baked in an earth oven, steamed, or boiled. My favorite preparation is slices of the fruit fried in oil—crisp, greasy, and delicious.

To the Butaritari, the most important food is the enormous, tuberous swamp taro or *babai*. The plants grow in deep pits carved out of the coral surface and extending down into the water lens. This is the only crop intensively farmed on the island. Each stem is carefully planted, weeded, and fed with vegetable humus held in place by coconut or pandanus leaves woven into a wreath around the base. The plants grow high, shadowing even tall people with their thick, fleshy leaves. In the Butaritari scheme, fourteen types of *babai* are recognized, falling into the two main categories of feasting and everyday tubers. The large tubers that do not self-propagate are grown for public, ceremonial events; the smaller, self-propagating forms are eaten as a regular part of household meals. The fibrous, gray flesh of cooked taro is the most prestigious food, which must be offered in large quantities during important celebrations. As a measure of the value placed on *babai,* when I had a chance to examine the photos I took on Butaritari, I found I had more pictures of piles of *babai* corms than anything else. At any celebration people wanted me to take as many photos of the roots as possible to remind everyone of the impressive size of their taro offerings.

Pigs and chickens, the two domesticated animals in the diet, are eaten only on festive occasions. Chickens peck their way freely through the village, and pigs are kept on the edge of the residential section tied with a rope to one of their back legs, to be fattened on household leftovers. Dogs and cats run semi-wild in the village, feeding on scraps and scavenging from kitchens. I heard of a couple of cases on more southerly atolls of roasted dog being served at parties, but I never saw it being eaten on Butaritari.

The limited number of staple crop foods gives the diet a lack of variety. For me, a typical evening meal was fresh tuna fried over a kerosene stove, accompanied by the ubiquitous mound of cold, sticky rice, sometimes with a slice of fibrous, boiled swamp taro or half a papaya. The Butaritari are very content with a diet of swamp taro, fish, rice, and toddy. They eat with gusto, in large quantity, and often, saying they eat very well. And to eat well, according to the local saying, is to live well.

Rice, tea, matches, flour, kerosene, batteries, and tobacco make up the imported necessities of contemporary Butaritari life. Households need to find small, regular amounts of cash to purchase these from the tiny stores that dot the island. Some households rely on remittances sent from sons working on foreign sea vessels or mining phosphate in nearby Nauru. Others sell copra, the dried flesh of the coconut, to the government for sale to international markets. Tuna and bananas can bring in cash when they are sent to Tarawa to be sold there.

Even with the need to find cash for the small list of imported necessities, the workload on Butaritari is relatively light for everyone, including the women. All household members contribute the work that needs to be done for the household, and time spent in all forms of work (farming, domestic, volunteer) accounts for less than half of the twelve daylight hours for all ages and both genders. The Butaritari pity the lifestyle they say people have on other atolls, where "they are so poor they have to work more than they rest." In unallocated time, Butaritari adults nap, gossip, play cards, listen to the radio, sing, joke, and tell stories.

Economic activities are differentiated by gender, with men focused on outdoor activities and women in the household. Men's and women's work tend to be different: Women care for the children, clean, cook, collect shellfish in the lagoon, weave, and sew. Men fish, work on boats, climb coconut trees, and farm taro. These distinctions are not hard and fast, though—women farm and fish, and men may help around the house and care for children. However, only a man can cut the flower spathe of the coconut to obtain toddy.

Toddy cutting takes place early in the morning and evening. The skill and magic surrounding toddy cutting are carefully guarded, and the secrets are passed among men of the same family as a special inheritance. The household toddy cutter is most often and appropriately young and unmarried. The young men grasp containers formed from hollow coconut shells or glass bottles and limber lithely up the coconut trunks, toddy knife held buccaneerlike in the teeth. To produce toddy the unopened flower spathe of the coconut is bound tightly with coconut-fiber string, and a cut is made that allows the sap to drip into the container hung off the spathe. Toddy cutters often sing melodically and almost hauntingly while they work in the trees, and their

A deaf and almost blind woman uses a wooden mallet to soften pandanus for weaving, then rolls it into working skeins.

voices carry out across the island at dusk and dawn. The local tradition tells that toddy cutters were made to sing so women bathing below would know they could be seen.

Each cutter may be tending three to four plants simultaneously, with a good palm producing more than a liter of toddy each day. Toddy is popular fresh, especially for children, or boiled into a sweet, sticky syrup (rather like Aunt Jemima's) to use as a base for drinks or to pour over food. If fresh toddy is left in an unwashed coconut shell for several days, a cidery, sour brew is formed that has the alcohol content of a weak wine.

Arguably the most persistently contentious social issue in Butaritari is alcohol abuse. Men's sour-toddy drinking parties may start early in the morning and last noisily into the night, and drunk men are a common sight in Butaritari village. I had an early introduction to male drunkenness on Butaritari: I arrived for the first time at the village clinic and found nobody there except a drunk man trussed up like a pig and slung across the clinic entrance attempting, somewhat comically and with little success, to untangle himself. Drunkenness is sometimes punished or controlled through such informal means; in this case the village medical officer had taken it upon himself to lasso the troublemaker until he was sober. Some islands in the Tungaru chain are "dry" and have more substantial social sanctions against drunkenness, and this has significantly curtailed male insobriety around villages. Village meetings and celebrations in Butaritari are most often alcohol-free events. However, broken legs are common from men falling off their secret drinking perches in coconut trees.

Men working in a household garden.

THE *MANEABA*

The social rounds in the village focus on church activities and are centered in the meeting house or *maneaba*—a large, beautifully constructed, rectangular building, with a steeply pitched roof supported by large blocks of coral rock. Huge, impressive feasts accompany all family and village celebrations: marriages, first birthdays, funerals. At such celebrations the floor of the *maneaba* becomes covered with such feast foods as whole pig, piles of cooked lobster, chicken, copious amounts and varieties of fish, giant clams and crabs, fish marinated in toddy vinegar with coconut milk, sea turtle, and the most important of all feast foods—mounds of large swamp taro.

After the feast, the *maneaba* is cleared of food, and the entertainment begins in earnest. Formal dancing troupes wear uniforms of matching lavalava, a rectangular cloth worn like a skirt and often complexly embroidered with a group symbol or name. Solo dancing women wear intricately knotted grass skirts, which are smoked and scented and rustle attractively as they move.

Young men wear finely woven mats for special dances. They are pulled around the waist and secured with a long, twisted lock of women's hair—often from the grandmother—that has magical properties or with a belt of coconut fiber. Dancers are rubbed with coconut oil to give their skin a sheen and are powdered and perfumed to make them smell strongly sweet. This smell protects the dancer from the malicious influence of spirits while they are in the "vulnerable" emotional state that emerges from a powerful performance. Sometimes arm and finger bands are worn, which exaggerate and accent the controlled movements of the most difficult dances.

Men work cooperatively to raise a new maneaba.

More general group dancing is boisterous, with a slapping, shuffling format. The group has a wide repertoire of dancing styles, all accompanied by a rasping, rapid a cappella from the crowd. These dancing occasions are moving and beautiful, rich with an emotion that pulls the observer along. Certainly, the sweep of emotion involved in these dances left me in tears more than once.

After the formal dancing, "te twist" gets going—meaning dancing to rock and roll, reggae, and pop music. The dancing is energetic, sometimes intentionally comic and, once the elder women become involved, overtly sexual. This is well-illustrated with an extract from my diary:

> After the feast and the formal dancing, the floor of the *maneaba* was cleared, a tape deck materialized and the crowd got to join the dancing. Being the only *I Matang,* I was *bubuti'd* [an irrefusable request] immediately to dance, and trotted up to entertain the crowd with my extremely subdued version of the lambada—which today was top-of-the-pops and was played repeatedly all afternoon. I got great cheers each time my partner dipped me, which became more often with each cheer. Soon my somewhat dull attempts at dancing and the more boisterous "twist" of the other young folk were replaced by the old women. Today they were singularly intent on the obscene—always a crowd-pleaser. One [older woman] specialized in pelvic thrusts in time to the music, another in spraying perfume into the crotches of dancing men. The performance that whipped the crowd into a frenzy was when Bauro* [a married man in his forties] somehow managed to coerce Kime* [his nephew's wife's aunt in her fifties] into dancing with him and got on all fours over her and simulated some highly imaginative sexual positions—all the time managing to stay in time to the music and punctuating the performance with some comically exaggerated lustful facial expressions. I found myself carried along with the crowd and laughing so hard my stomach was in knots. It was a fabulous afternoon's entertainment. (Field Journal, November 5, 1990)

The *maneaba* is also used as the arena for village discussions, debates among the elders, and group decision making. Each family has an inherited place on the *maneaba* floor, where their representative sits during discussions. However, this is a recently developed pattern of family representation begun under a colonial hand since the demise of the kingship.

CONTROL OF LAND

Until the turn of the century, the northern islands of Makin and Butaritari together comprised a separate political unit from the rest of the Gilbert chain. The cohesion of the political unit was maintained by extensive internal kinship ties and a chiefly or kingly line, headed by the *uea* or king, who had ultimate authority over the area. Given the enduring role land plays in Butaritari society, the real power of the *uea* lay in his control of land use on both Makin and Butaritari. The *uea* title was inherited, usually by an eldest son, with the other close relatives forming the aristocracy.

Commoners could release themselves from servitude to the king and his lands by entering "linkage" relationships with the king, a special reciprocal relationship generated by providing the king with another wife and by her bearing children. In this way, commoner families had much to gain from producing daughters and keeping them chaste for a royal marriage. A linked family would be expected, in return for the release from servitude to the king, to provide feast food and hospitality whenever called on to do so.

The British colonial government moved to abolish the *uea* title in 1963. The traditional autocratic power of the kingship had, however, already been undermined significantly in 1922 when the colonial administration completely reorganized the land tenure system, taking households that had been dispersed as hamlets in the bush and lining them up in villages along a central thoroughfare. At this time control over village and family activities started to move to the heads of families. The Council of Elders, comprised of all the senior family heads, is now responsible for overseeing village and island affairs, with the administrative posts provided by the island council under the umbrella of the central government.

With the demise of the kingship, the newer ethos of Butaritari sense of reciprocity and obligation is decidedly more egalitarian, at least in theory—although kingly families retain a self-styled elitism. People see themselves, and their households, acting as semi-autonomous and self-interested units, rather than first and foremost providing loyalty to the village community.

A vital and potent social unit in Butaritari society, the *utu,* is all those people who are linked to each other as kin and who share common ownership of land plots. Everyone on the island belongs to several *utu;* they may inherit the land rights for each from either parent. For this reason, to marry a child to another with access to much land is advantageous to a family, because it will increase the land holding of the family when the grandchild becomes a recipient of inherited land from the spouse married into the family.

Kinship lines are traced through shared rights to land. Those who have the greatest control of any piece of land, though, are those who live on that piece of land. The *kainga,* or family estate, sits at the heart of each *utu,* and those who live on the particular *kainga* of one of their *utu* have the greatest say in *utu* affairs and the largest share of any produce from the land held in that *utu*. In these ways, access to and ownership of land is the theme that underlies and cements all social relations.

Children also are valuable for the links they provide to other families, particularly other families as landowning units. Producing and raising children is economically important to a couple. A growing daughter provides valuable assistance around the house; a young son can cut the toddy. The childless woman or man in Butaritari society is pitied and treated as somehow childlike.

The social value of children as potential inheritors of land is best exemplified by the pragmatic land-for-children transfers that take place when couples decide to adopt out children to other families. Children can be adopted by other family members or friends of the family in either the position of "grandchild" or "child." Child adoption is more common, and the child will move to live with a family and become a sibling to the other children in the family. This form of adoption confers real benefits to the child. The child is now considered to have two sets of parents and gains the benefits of both sets of parents, including rights to use of and inheritance of land. The reasons for effecting an adoption are often blatantly economic from the parents' point of view. The family providing the child for adoption will be passed land in exchange. The adoption is not considered binding until the land changes hands. Where a child is adopted for especially emotive reasons, such as to fill the gap left by a dead child or to provide children for an infertile couple, they will be especially spoiled. Generally, adopted children can be expected to be treated preferentially over natural-born children, and the natural parents can claim back a child if they suspect the child is being treated improperly.

RELIGION

Catholicism pervades many aspects of Butaritari life. Many *maneaba* on the island are owned by the churches, and the majority of Butaritari are Catholic (80 percent). But Christianity has not completely supplanted a belief in other supernatural forces; magic is still an important part of healing, love, and performance arts, and it is impossible to discuss misfortune without reference to the mischievous *anti* or spirits that share the atoll with the living.

As in other parts of the Pacific, Butaritari was the site of a scrappy and venomous struggle between Catholic and Protestant missionaries for converts. It was under the guardianship of early trader Richard Randell that the first Christian service was held on the island in 1852. However, the first mission station was not established until 1865, when two protestant Hawai'ian missionaries were sent there to "convert the heathens." That particular mission was short-lived—the missionaries fled the country in fear for their lives. They had been present when king Na Kaeia executed three Hawai'ian seamen. According to missionary records, the king became incensed after the captain of a trading ship threw a coconut at the king's cousin, and the king climbed on the seamen's backs and slit their throats. The Butaritari oral tradition tells a similar story, adding the postscript that the sailors also were eaten. Later missionary work proceeded more smoothly, with the main thrust of the missionary campaigns focused on curtailing rather than eliminating the more intractable "pagan customs" of polygyny (multiple wives), dancing, and drinking.

By the 1890s the competition between the Catholic and Protestant churches for converts became more earnest. Each congregation fell in and out of public favor as each side managed to convert a series of kings from one religion to another. Finally, the Catholics gained a real advantage by managing to convert the entire Butaritari aristocracy to Catholicism at once. Since this time, Catholicism has been the dominant nominal religion on Butaritari, although a Protestant enclave exists in Kuma village in the northeast. The Protestant mission temporarily abandoned the island in 1901 after labeling the island as "the darkest and most discouraging in the Pacific," presumably because the Catholic mission proved so successful.

I MATANG

Although missionaries had an early and significant influence in the historic transformation of Butaritari society, they were not the first Europeans to locate and live on the island. The first European to sight Butaritari may have been the Spanish explorer Pedro Fernández de Quirós, who sailed through the area early in 1606. But it was not until more than a century and a half later that the island was sketched on a European map. The first formal chart of Butaritari and other atolls in the chain was made by the United States Exploring Expedition in 1841. This group had a short but well-recorded visit to the island, writing that by 1835 three *I Matang* had been living on Butaritari, one of whom was a colorful Scot called Robert Wood who left a whaling ship some seven years earlier. Wood well may have been the first *I Matang* to interact with the locals—indicated by his report that when he first arrived on Butaritari, he was carried about on people's shoulders for several months. Castaway "Bob" is credited with the dubious distinction of introducing fermentation techniques to the island, demonstrating how to transform coconut toddy into its intoxicating sour form.

From 1840 to 1870 whaling vessels called at Butaritari frequently, most often to boil down blubber and seduce local women. Unlike other atolls in the group, Butaritari has a deep and open lagoon that allows large sailing ships to moor safely. Although the mooring was easy, the seduction was not—at least compared to the purported friendliness of Eastern Polynesian women—and the sailors quickly turned their sexual attention elsewhere in the Pacific.

From the 1840s to the 1880s at least a dozen *I Matang* traders were living on the island at any time, exchanging iron, tobacco, and trinkets for coconut oil, copra, turtle shell, and *bêche-de-mer*—an edible sea cucumber still considered a delicacy to Asian palates. The most powerful trader was Randell, who set up alliances with the Butaritari king. Randell's marital prowess speaks of the status he managed to achieve on the island: He had at least four simultaneous wives, including the daughter of a high chief, during his years on the island.

The raising of the Union Jack on the island in 1892 signaled the imposition of the British protectorate. After trade in coconut oil slacked in the late 1800s, the European traders moved away. The long-term impact of the traders on Butaritari as arbiters of social change was limited despite several decades of close interaction, most particularly because prevailing social pressure forced them to conform to Butaritari lifestyle—bowing to the king's whims and taking several local wives (on the whole, they seem to have been happy with this arrangement).

Through the first few decades of this century, Butaritari became an increasingly global backwater—holding no resources of interest to *I Matang* markets and becoming one of the more obscure corners of the British empire. Kiribati became a British colony in 1916, an arrangement that endured until 1979, when the country finally achieved independence.

Since the traders left, few *I Matang* have been living on the island, mainly occasional missionaries, Peace Corps volunteers, and anthropologists.

By far the most dramatic episode in the history of contact between Butaritari and *I Matang* was the Japanese occupation of the island during World War II, followed by a dramatic liberation of the island by American Marines. Several hundred Japanese troops landed on the island in late 1941, intending it to be a handy seaplane base for the Japanese westward advance across the Pacific toward Hawai'i. Despite the occupation, the island was quiet for the next seven months. Children attended Japanese schools, and local work parties were formed. In August 1942, two American submarines loaded with marines, sent by a U.S. war administration desperate for any successful incursions into Japanese occupied territory, arrived off the coast of Butaritari village. In the course of the ensuing raid, all the occupying Japanese were killed, along with thirty U.S. Marines and one Butaritari. The Americans withdrew promptly, but the Japanese—thinking incorrectly the island was now under American occupation—sent out a bombing sortie several days later. All three planes misidentified their target in Butaritari village and dropped their bomb load on the village of Keuea. Keuea ceased to exist—although the village was rebuilt at a new site later—and the island death records show at least forty-five villagers died as a result of the bombing. The Japanese promptly reoccupied the island, and the tenor of the occupation became harsher. The occupation force was larger, and the execution of a Butaritari man later that month is recorded in the death register.

On November 20, 1943, the U.S. Marines launched an all-out attack on Butaritari to coincide with their storming of Tarawa to the south. In four days of fighting, almost 300 Japanese soldiers and 271 of their Japanese and Korean laborers—the entire contingent—were killed or captured. Nine villagers also were killed in the battle, three of whom died in a hail of bullets they probably would have avoided had they not been drunk at the time. The matériel remains of that conflict still scatter the reef and beaches of the island: downed seaplanes rest in the lagoon, bomb craters and foxholes are found throughout Butaritari village. Marine dog tags and shell casings still can be picked up from the ground. In all, more than fifty-five thousand coconut trees were downed in the Japanese–American conflict, and many *babai* pits were destroyed by bombs. Despite the level of crop destruction, including many breadfruit trees dying, nothing in the historic record indicates any particular hardship over the next years. The most lasting, tangible impact of the contact with Japanese may have been both a proliferation of herbal medicines since World War II and an enduring taste for rice.

However, the war experience has been important in forging how Butaritari see their relationship to the world beyond. My stay coincided with the Gulf War crisis of

The remains of World War II Japanese defense structures still dominate sections of the Tarawa shoreline..

1991. In the lead-up to the January 15 "deadline" for Saddam Hussein's withdrawal from Kuwait, everyone on Butaritari showed an extraordinary interest in the developments in the Middle East. I would be asked each day to describe the BBC newscasts in detail, and for several weeks all conversations focused on the Gulf. People from other islands talked about traveling home, and prisoners held on Tarawa petitioned the government to be reunited with their families. These responses to the Gulf War initially surprised me, since I felt the opposite—I probably was safer in isolated Kiribati than anywhere else. It became evident to me as the discussions progressed that the feelings of threat from the Gulf War crisis stemmed from the World War II experience. The Butaritari were fearful that while the eyes of the world were turned elsewhere (as they were to Europe in World War II), other powers would take the opportunity to seize Kiribati, just as the Japanese had done.

DISEASE

The incursions of global conflict into Butaritari is not how the greatest impact of *I Matang* contact has been felt on Butaritari, however. As in many other parts of the Pacific, contact with *I Matang* guaranteed contact with the diseases they carried, and these have had an important, if negative, place in the unfolding history of the island. In looking at ecological history, it is possible to trace how contact with *I Matang* transformed Butaritari health.

In many regions, such as Central and North America, Hawai'i, Australia, and New Zealand, the first decades of contact with Europeans proved frighteningly lethal for local groups as they came into contact with diseases with which they had no prior exposure. The two new diseases that killed the greatest number of people in the early years of *I Matang* contact on Butaritari were influenza and dysentery, often complicated by measles. Kanoa, one of the Hawai'ian Protestant missionaries on Butaritari, wrote of a "great epidemic" in 1866, in which at least 85 died, that was likely to have been influenza. At the time probably about 1,500 to 2,000 people were living on the island.

Bacillary dysentery, a bacterial disease transmitted in the water supply that results in severe stomach cramps and diarrhea, was repeatedly introduced by contact with crews of sailing ships the past century. Infection has become more common since several cess-pit toilets were built in Butaritari village, all precariously close to the well-water supply. Around a quarter of all people in Butaritari village are treated in the clinic each year for dysentery, and I was infected several times while on the island—although it is now treatable with antibiotics.

It was not only waterborne disease that came on each ship but also the sexually transmitted diseases common among European crews. Sexually transmitted diseases were not present in the chain before the arrival of *I Matang,* but outbreaks of gonorrhea ("the clap") certainly followed. Captain Davis, arriving by ship in 1892, writes that he dropped a gonorrhea-infected man on the island who was being repatriated from the Marshall Islands. He tried hard to convince the king that the man was a health threat, but, with little experience of the disease, Davis claims the king found his requests for sexual quarantine merely amusing.

Gonorrhea is caused by a bacterium and is very easily spread in sexual contact. Because the disease puts women at risk of severe pelvic infection, it can cause infertility in women. Estimating the extent of childlessness in these island populations is a reasonably reliable, if indirect, means of tracing past episodes of gonorrhea. The evidence from Butaritari is ambiguous in this regard. Some indication in genealogies is that fertility was lower in the latter half of the nineteenth century, but the extent of childlessness is difficult to gauge. Generally, in the northern part of the Tungaru chain, at least, no widespread childlessness occurred, and widespread infection with gonorrhea can be ruled out. One reason the disease may not have spread widely was the particular internal arrangement of Butaritari sexual "networking"—where unmarried, sexually available women were few in number and not nearly as sexually available as visiting European sailors would have liked.

Syphilis, a potentially lethal and disfiguring sexually transmitted disease if untreated, was common in Europe but rare in Butaritari through these first decades of European contact in the Pacific. Butaritari, wet and warm, lies within the "yaws zone" of the Pacific—the region where the tropical, ulcerous, but nonlethal disease of yaws was present since at least 1860, and maybe even in the precontact period. By 1920 all adults and most children were affected with yaws. The disease shares a similar bacterial basis with syphilis, and childhood infection with yaws provides an effective cross-immunity against syphilis. A history of yaws was an epidemiological blessing in disguise.

In many parts of the Pacific, the impact of European diseases was apocalyptic. For example, on the small outlying Polynesian atoll of Nukuoro, some 70 percent of the population died in a mere forty years, and on the Western Micronesian island of Yap the population collapsed when well more than half of the adult women became sterile from venereal diseases. Comparatively speaking, Butaritari fared well. The overall death rate from acute infectious diseases was not as large on Butaritari as it was elsewhere in the Pacific. Sylvester Lambert, a widely traveled physician who visited the Tungaru chain in the 1920s with the Rockefeller Foundation International Health Commission to seek and treat hookworm, wrote that the people in the Tungaru chain were then the healthiest people in the Pacific and that "the white colonists of the Gilberts needed a doctor more than the natives" (1941:190). This was an advantage of relative isolation—Tungaru being hard to locate, far from the most important *I Matang* trade routes, short of resources valued by *I Matang* consumers, and, with the exception of Butaritari, having no decent ports. Butaritari ability to withstand these new diseases also reflected the generally adequate health status—better nourished groups are better armed to fight disease.

In the early historic years of the kingship, nutrition was more than adequate most of the time. The diet provided regular fat from coconuts, protein from fish, and calories from toddy. According to early *I Matang* writings, Butaritari were legendarily large and wide, causing European observers in the late nineteenth century to describe some as a "moving mass of jelly." The king and his family ate voraciously, even being force-fed on pre-chewed food and gallons of fresh toddy. Not only was food plentiful, but also endemic disease was minimal. The debilitating parasitic disease filariasis did not exist, which causes massive swellings in breasts, groin, and legs and was well known in Tuvalu to the south. There was, and still is, no malaria.

But the introduction and spread of tuberculosis (TB) changed this picture of reasonable health for the worse. The disease was most likely first introduced by workers returning from the phosphate mines on Nauru, and by the 1930s it accounted for more than a third of all deaths in the Tungaru chain. Tuberculosis has been the biggest killer in the Pacific this century, and the disease continues to ravage, waste, and kill—the TB ward at the central hospital in Tarawa is often full. TB rates on Butaritari historically have been the lowest in the chain. This is most likely because a comparatively better diet on the atoll provided both greater protection against catching the infection and against the disease progressing.

The traditional diet, if adequate, was not and still is not ideal. The main dietary deficiency is vitamin A. A lack of this essential vitamin can cause night blindness and eventual corneal damage and total blindness. Even mild deficiencies of vitamin A can put children at greater risk of respiratory disease and diarrhea, both of which are very common causes of illness and death in Butaritari children. A survey of 4,000 schoolchildren through the country in 1990 found some 15 percent had notable signs of vitamin A deficiency. Sweet potato, a root crop very high in the vitamin A precursor of beta-carotene, is eaten everywhere else in the Pacific except for Kiribati. Vitamin A is also released from green vegetables when they are eaten with fats such as coconut cream, although green vegetables are scorned on Butaritari as pig food.

Other health problems that have a long history on the island include parasitic infection from various intestinal worms. Hookworm is a particularly insidious parasite spread by contact with human feces. Eggs carried in the feces hatch on moist soil to produce larvae able to penetrate the skin of human feet. In the human host they bind to the stomach lining and begin to bleed their victim, sucking the host of nutrients. Hookworms thrive in such rainier climates as Butaritari, where the larvae can survive longer outside a host. The traditional defecation pattern, below the water on the lagoon beach, is one way parasitic load is kept down—the tidal change cleans the area twice daily.

When a physician named O'Connor visited the island in 1920, he found that one-fifth of the people were found infected with hookworm and more than two-thirds with whipworm *(Trichuris)*. Whipworm is still common. It is transmitted mainly when people use their hands to eat, as is the custom on Butaritari. Like hookworms, whipworms deprive the host of iron, making the victim anemic. A complex, synergistic relationship between anemia and susceptibility to infection and diarrhea exists. The iron-poor nature of the soils on the atoll means a low iron intake in the diet, which adds further to the anemia problem, and intense anemia makes it harder for affected people to fight other infections.

In recent years a number of "new" diseases have started to take a severe health toll. Hepatitis B, a viral disease that begins with an inflamed liver and can end in death, is widespread on Butaritari, infecting upwards of 95 percent of the people at some time in their lives (see Table 1-1). In the United States the disease is most often spread through contact with body fluids during sex—in much the same manner as HIV, the virus that causes AIDS. On Butaritari the disease is not transmitted sexually; rather, it is passed within the family early in life, most often from child-to-child in saliva, blood, and the large, weepy ulcers that commonly fester on legs. The virus that causes the disease is a very potent carcinogen. Aggravated by alcohol and tobacco, liver cancer is a major killer of young Butaritari men, who also suffer high rates of alcohol-associated cirrhosis, or liver degeneration.

Kiribati has one of the highest smoking rates in the world, with two-thirds of adult women smoking and up to 90 percent of adult men. Thick, pungent tobacco, imported from Papua New Guinea, is shaved with a razor blade off a leafy twist to be tapped onto a rectangle of dry pandanus leaf and rolled into a cigarette. The pandanus leaf burns slowly and inefficiently, and a couple of cigarettes can be made to last a whole day. Smoking is popular both for the pleasure people say it brings and for the association it has with being "grown-up." According to a dentist on Tarawa, oral cancer is surprisingly rare, and hospital records show few deaths from lung cancer. Likely, it is not immunity from the health effects of smoking; rather, life expectancy is so low that people fail to live long enough to develop any symptoms.

The transformation of Butaritari health over the last 150 years has been predominantly the result of contact with *I Matang*—exposure to new diseases, the introduction of some Western dietary items, and the introduction of biomedical technology and a national health service. In the 1920s, life expectancy was about 40 years at birth. It is now about 50 years for men and 55 years for women. Much of this gain has been from a drop in infant death rates, rather than any real benefit in length of adult lives—even now, few people live beyond 65 years of age. Currently about 8 to

TABLE 1-1   THE CAUSES OF DEATH RECORDED BY BUTARITARI CLINIC STAFF
IN 1988 AND 1989

	Number Dying	
	Children Under Age Five	*Children Over Age 5 and Adults*
Malnutrition/diarrhea	6	0
Meningitis	3	0
Bronchitis/pneumonia	2	2
Choking/suffocation	2	0
Fish poisoning	2	0
Abdominal pain/peritonitis	1	3
Hepatitis/cirrhosis	1	3
Heart attack	0	1
"Old age"	0	1
Peptic ulcer	0	1
Stab wound	0	2

The causes of death recorded by Butaritari clinic staff in 1988 and 1989. Fish poisoning is a common cause of illness. One in eighty people nationally are treated each year in the clinics for poisoning by ciguatera or salmonella. Both stab-wound victims were young men.

10 percent of children die in the first year of life, most often from diarrheas. This is one of the highest infant death rates in the Pacific region. Overall, the Butaritari have not seen the gains in health that many other groups in the region have as they have come into contact with Western medicine and changed sanitary practices—which is especially poignant, given that only sixty years ago Sylvestor Lambert wrote they were "the most healthy in the Pacific" (1941:190).

The situation may soon change, though. Infant vaccination programs are currently well-organized and reach almost all children on the island. I tagged along on several immunization drives and was impressed with the turnout of local mothers and children. Even with the logistic problems of transport and with keeping the vaccines fresh without refrigeration, the clinic staff manage to immunize upward of 90 percent of the children against a wide range of diseases—tuberculosis, diphtheria, polio, whooping cough, tetanus, measles, and hepatitis B.

POPULATION

In examining the modern history of the island, one way to find a crystallization of ecologically important events is to look at affected population numbers and the rate of population growth or decline. Variation in population numbers on the island corresponds well to periods of the introduction and spread of introduced diseases. Disease was not only implicated, though. The population stopped growing through the second half of the past century, despite fertility being high. Between 1850 and 1880, slave traders or "blackbirders" were responsible for kidnapping hundreds from the Tungaru islands for forced labor in the plantations of the Pacific, Australia, and Mexico, and the guano mines of Peru. The Butaritari seem to have been spared the brunt of the recruitment activities, if only because of their reputation as "troublesome workers"; however, at least several hundred people were lost from the island. After 1880 the colonial government finally introduced some protective measures against the blackbirders.

The population numbers stayed relatively stable between the turn of the century and the 1920s. Population growth slowed briefly through the years of occupation in World War II and in the early 1970s, when biomedical contraceptives (The Pill and intrauterine devices) were introduced. Otherwise, numbers have been increasing steadily since the 1930s (see Figure 5).

Groups living on islands with finite land-based resources depend at some time on reasonably effective means to limit the number of people, either deliberate or not. Classic ecological approaches often have chosen to demonstrate how human small-scale, nonindustrial populations have developed a homeostatic relationship between human activity and the successful and sustained exploitation of the environment in which that activity occurs. In such cases, it is often posed that success depends on balance, particularly a balance of numbers of people in relation to resources. To maintain that balance, checks on population may be internal and more personal

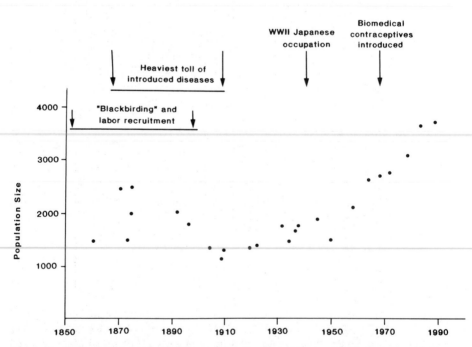

Figure 5   Estimates of population size on Butaritari by explorers, missionaries, and later government censuses, finishing with my own census in late 1990. Tracing the history of changes in population size on Butaritari shows the effects of important events—the "black-birding" and introduction of infectious diseases in the past century and the Japanese occupation of World War II. The shortfall of the growth rate in the late 1960s corresponds with the introduction of biomedical contraceptives. The population has been growing steadily since about 1920 and continues to do so today.

(infanticide, abortion, contraception) or external and often accidental (warfare, earthquake, disease). The homeostasis argument does not rightly apply in Butaritari, at least not in the sense I have stated it here: In the past 150 years, the period of recorded history, the population was fluctuating more than it was maintained at a static or semi-stable level.

Generally, human population sizes are subject to controls both directly and indirectly, whether or not a limitation is deliberately imposed. On islands, where resource limits can make numerically large populations difficult to sustain, population control, by whatever form, can emerge as a vital, practical issue. This generally does not happen as an organized, collective effort, however. Rather, population regulation is an incidental result of individuals and couples making decisions, consciously or not, that have an outcome in keeping population size down. The means for dealing with the stresses of overpopulation are varied, including migrating, although drawing conceptual lines between various activities and an adaptive system of population regulation is very tricky, if not impossible. That is, it is easy to show that a particular behavioral complex—such as warfare or emigration—functions to keep population numbers down, but it is difficult to argue clearly that such is the sole adaptive or functional purpose of warring or migration activities.

The question of whether Tungaru population numbers stayed fairly stable before *I Matang* arrival is difficult to address because so little prehistoric archaeology has been done in the northern atolls. It does appear, though, that the population had some room for expansion still available in the late prehistoric and early historic era, through the first half of the 1800s. Large tracts of land were uncultivated, filled with wild, scrappy salt-bush trees in 1841. Wood made detailed statements to the Exploring Expedition about the ease of life on Butaritari at that time, particularly in comparison to the harder lives on islands farther south, and Wilkes wrote "Wood accounts for their [relative corpulence] by their being at all times abundantly well supplied with food, and leading an inactive life" (1856,V:83). The inference of these early historic accounts, given that the island already had been settled for about fifteen hundred years, is that some form of successful population regulation was in effect that kept enough resources available to support a greedy and consumptive elite.

In some small-scale societies, warfare has been argued to have developed as an indirect mechanism to control population size. Warfare does not figure largely in Butaritari oral history and is unlikely to have been important in controlling population numbers at the end of the precontact period. The Butaritari kings kept a fairly tight rein on factional disputes, and the introduction of firearms in the mid-1800s—which led to bloody battles and countless deaths on islands farther south—appears to have been fairly peaceful.

However, several dynamic mechanisms have been in operation that prevented fertility ever reaching anything near a biological maximum on Butaritari Atoll. Before the turn of the century, men without land or the younger brothers of chiefs were prevented from marrying. Although adult women apparently outnumbered men, some commoner men were left without partners and so without children. Before the church missionaries cracked down on "pagan customs," men in chiefly classes could marry several women at once—the preferred pattern being to marry sets of sisters successively. According to Wilkes, writing in 1841, the king had upward of sixty

TABLE 1-2   MARRIAGE AND FERTILITY FIGURES FOR BUTARITARI

Age Group	Number of Women	Percentage Ever Married	Percentage Ever Married with at Least One Child	Average Number of Children per Ever-Married Women
15–19	109	39.4	65.1	0.77
20–24	158	83.5	87.1	1.69
25–29	134	93.3	95.2	2.95
30–34	117	98.3	97.4	4.10
35–39	84	100.0	98.1	5.48
40–44	62	98.4	95.1	5.67
45–49	56	100.0	100.0	5.79
50 +	176	95.5	98.3	7.57

Marriage and fertility figures for Butaritari, based on a census of 896 women in November 1990. The average size of completed families—that is, the number of children a woman has by the time she reaches menopause—is six to eight children.

wives and concubines, although genealogical records, taken in the 1960s by anthropologist Bernd Lambert, set the upper limit to around twelve formally wed wives to one king. In fact, the polygynous system persisted quietly until very recently. Betsy Sewell, an anthropologist living on the island in the early 1970s, recorded at that time at least one man on the island married polygynously. And, currently, the most popular replacement wives for a widowed man are his polygynous wives by tradition—the sisters of his wife.

Delayed age at marriage is a well-recognized mechanism for controlling fertility in the absence of contraceptive behavior. According to the observations of 1930s colonial officer Arthur Grimble, who spoke the language and took great efforts to record local oral tradition, men married at higher ages in the previous century. The series of ordeals that tested and prepared a boy for adulthood and for marriage did not begin until chest hair was obvious, at about twenty-three years of age. It then would be at least another three years until the man was qualified as a warrior and so as a husband. The age for first marriages dropped through this century but has changed little over the last several decades. It is currently just under twenty for women and about twenty-three for men. Combined with a social emphasis on premarital virginity, few women have their first birth before they reach age twenty (see Table 1-2). This is another indirect method of fertility regulation.

Infanticide, killing newborns to keep families smaller, has been used widely as a "birth-control method" throughout most of human history. In the island groups of the Pacific, early European explorer accounts make it clear that infanticide was widespread throughout the region. On Butaritari, oral tradition tells that newborns were occasionally smothered or buried. It is difficult to establish how common the practice was, because any public mention disappeared rapidly once *I Matang* colonial and church officers were on the island. Both showed disapproval, the missionaries particularly thinking it a "moral duty" to stop the practice. However, the value of children for forging adoptive relationships makes it likely infanticide was not common, and this is supported by the oral tradition. Wood told Captain Wilkes he had never heard of a case after living seven years on the island.

Abortion by traditional means was widespread through the years of early *I Matang* contact, though, and still occurs occasionally. The practice seems to have increased in the same period infanticide was being curtailed by colonial law, and it is tempting to speculate a causal connection. If early *I Matang* reports can be trusted, in the early historic period abortion was done by married women as well as by single women. Abortion was made illegal, punishable with life imprisonment, very early in the colonial period. I spent several days sieving through pre-independence court documents in Tarawa and failed to find records of any case coming to trial in the islands of Tungaru. Reliable evidence must have been very difficult for British prosecutors to obtain, so women were generally safe from prosecution. The most common, and effective, abortion method practiced on Butaritari today is hard abdominal massage supplemented with locally prepared herbal drinks. I interviewed several women who had aborted by choice, helped by female kin, using these traditional techniques. All of them had been unmarried at the time and were ashamed of the pregnancy. The act is still illegal, although most Butaritari women are unaware this is the case.

Spurred by fears of imminent overpopulation, mostly in response to high population growth rates, a government family-planning campaign began in 1968 and included free fitting of intrauterine devices (IUDs) or packets of oral contraceptives (The Pill). Although many women were quick to try the new methods, popularity of the new methods rapidly waned. Now, despite contraceptives being widely available and free, Butaritari fertility is barely lower now than it was in the decades before the introduction of biomedical contraceptives. In fact, Butaritari fertility measures are high, even when compared to other human groups in "relatively traditional" settings where biomedical contraceptives are not available.

Although death rates are high and life expectancy is low, the population of Butaritari is still growing because of high fertility—at a rapid rate of around 2.2 percent a year—which means the population will double in size in just more than thirty years if this rate endures (see Figure 6). In marked contrast to the government fears of overpopulation, the Butaritari seem *almost* unconcerned with the issue. When I asked people about the risks of running out of enough food for an expanding population, they would point to tracts of uncultivated land and the open sea and state they had little to worry about, at least for now. They patted their full stomachs and reminded me of the size of the *babai* mound at the last feast. And, should things change, they state, they had many options—such as moving some people to Tarawa or beyond. In fact, everyone had a pet plan for relocation. Said one middle-aged man:

> *I think they should move some people to Russia. I looked on the school map and there is so much room there, so much space. The big problem is I'm not so sure that coconut trees would grow well.*

The Butaritari, however, see a value in population numbers remaining relatively stable over time and talk positively about a hypothetical equilibrium, where the population would stop growing and a symmetrical pattern of landholding between generations would occur. Many speak disparagingly about the "Catholic rule" against birth control or click their tongues disapprovingly when discussing couples with large families.

What I have attempted to describe in this chapter is how, although Butaritari is an island, it has never been closed nor isolated, and contact with a wider world is

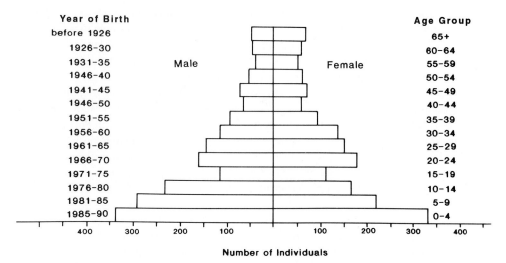

Figure 6   An age-sex pyramid for the whole atoll in November 1990. The total population size was 3,523, excluding the few families on the isolated islet of Bikati. The pyramid shows how "youthful" the population is, where children greatly outnumber adults. Few people live over age sixty-five. The shortage of both men and women in the fifteen-to-nineteen age group is temporary; many are attending secondary school on Tarawa. Most later return home.

hardly a recent phenomenon. In considering the ecological framework of life in Butaritari, it is valuable to develop a perspective that extends conceptually beyond the physical boundaries of the atoll and that considers human activity and experience within a broader sphere. On the other hand, it is vital to keep in mind the limitations of atoll life: the finiteness of space, resources, and opportunities for population expansion or intensification. It is these almost contradictory themes of isolation and contact that set the ecological and historical stage for better understanding women's lives, health, and sexuality—the topics of the next chapters.

2 / Women as Mothers and Lovers

NEI BWEBWEATA'S DAY

The first light arrives to the sounds of roosters and dogs, and pricks through the slatted coconut blinds onto the sleeping platform. Nei Bwebweata* rolls over on her mat, adjusts her lavalava over her dress, and twists her long hair back into a bun behind her head. Her young baby sleeps fitfully on a pillow beside her, protected by a mosquito net from the irksome flies and mosquitos.

Sitting up, she puts her young son to her breast and lets him take a sleepy drink. She is not the first to rise in the household. Although as senior married woman of the household she is in charge of its day-to-day running, she can allocate all the messiest, dullest, and earliest morning tasks to her sister, Kataua*. Younger and unmarried, Kataua has been staying with the family since the baby was born four months ago to help Bwebweata. Expected to work hard to demonstrate her marriageable qualities, Kataua is up first sweeping the compound, stoking the fire, and pulling water from the well.

Bwebweata prods her sleeping husband, Timon*, and passes him the baby, then ambles slowly toward the lagoon. She descends to the water's edge and relieves herself and wanders into the ocean for a quick wash. She potters back to the house and wraps herself in a fresh lavalava before heading to the kitchen hut to prepare a morning meal of leftovers and warm toddy for her eldest child, now three years old.

After breakfast, Bwebweata notices the sweeping is yet to be finished. She chides her sister for her laziness, telling her to stop resting and then see that the sleeping mats are spread in the sun. She takes the baby back up onto the platform as her husband starts collecting his lavalava around him in preparation for a morning in the taro pits. After a short bout of breastfeeding, Bwebweata lies down to nap next to the child, pulling herself under a mat so her nap will be uninterrupted. Her eldest child wanders off into the neighbor's house and joins a group of giggling children playing games with old cans, used batteries, and small stones.

While Bwebweata sleeps, Kataua walks to the beach to collect shellfish and worms. She returns around noon with a basket of small, fleshy clams dug from the lagoon sand at low tide with a piece of coconut shell, which are steamed for lunch. Everyone from the household joins in the lunch, including Timon, who had returned from the bush with a large babai *corm slung over each shoulder. The men eat first, served their clams and cold rice on the platform while Bwebweata and Kataua remain and snack with the children in the cooking house.*

After lunch, Timon rests on the platform. His eldest child leans against him as he slowly smokes a pandanus-leaf cigarette. As the baby sleeps beside her, Bwebweata gossips lazily with Kataua, who is sitting nearby and rolling coconut husk fiber into rope on her thigh. Eventually, everyone is napping.

After the early afternoon sting of heat has subsided, Timon walks to a meeting in the maneaba, *and Kataua goes to the edge of the bush with the eldest child to collect firewood. In the now quiet household, Bwebweata prepares some thatch, soaking pandanus leaves in water. Nearer dusk, Bwebweata's cousin arrives with two coconut shells full of toddy. Bwebweata greets her cousin with praise for the volume of his toddy and pours a measure into a plastic cup for her daughter to drink.*

Timon returns from the maneaba *with his cousin in tow, who has brought a fish to the family for dinner. While Kataua guts and fillets the fish and prepares to barbecue it over the kitchen fire, the two men sit cross-legged on the platform discussing the meeting. The baby is passed to Kataua, and Bwebweata replaces her in the cooking hut. She dishes out cold rice and more of the shellfish left from lunchtime, adds grated coconut, and serves the hot fish on large enamel plates. She presents these and two cups of toddy to the men and returns to the cooking hut to feed the children on fish, rice, and more toddy. It is important to have the serving done before the sunset so she does not need to waste the expense of lighting the kerosene lantern.*

Once the baby has been fed again and put to sleep and the daughter washed, dressed, and placed under a mosquito net, the men join the rest of the family around the fire. The adults laugh, sing, and tell stories together in the cooking hut. They nibble on leftovers, drink hot watered-down toddy syrup, and debate whether the conditions are right for catching flying fish this evening. It is decided that they will wait two days until full moon, when the fish will be more plentiful. People begin to float off into the dark, taking a full bath in the private blackness of night on the edges of the household before they retire. Cleaned and changed and sleek with coconut oil to keep her warm after the cool water of her bath, Bwebweata rolls back into her mats, feeds the baby one more time, and carefully checks that her daughter is completely covered with her mosquito net. As she begins to doze, her husband crawls onto her mat, fresh from his wash. They lie side by side and talk softly together for a few minutes, trying to decide which babai *they will harvest for a first birthday party the following week. This decided, they drift off to sleep.*

Although Butaritari days always strike me as relaxed and slow-paced—particularly compared to the hard and long hours of work that characterize subsistence agriculture in many parts of the world—when Butaritari women describe their lives, and their days, they most often talk about all the hard and busy work they do. This is a theme that emerges in many conversations with women—how they must work hard, harder than men; that they are by nature hard-working people; that work marks them as good and worthy wives and daughters; and that their work makes the household run, the *babai* grow, and their husbands happy. In the sections that follow, I trace this theme of hard women's work and two other themes that Butaritari women define as important in their lives: their relationships with their husbands and the violence that tests their bravery as women. In thinking conceptually about women's lives, these categories do not come to me as the most intellectually direct way to present an argument about an ecology of women; however, this format allows Butaritari women to define the contexts in which their sexuality, fertility, and health are described and analyzed in this book.

WORK IN WOMEN'S LIVES

Women fall into four primary categories in Butaritari society, which change as they marry and age: virgins, housewives, old women, and *nikiranroro*. The term *nikiranroro*

Three young cousins play together. Before puberty, girls have few responsibilities and spend much time in play with siblings and cousins.

is difficult to translate exactly into English, but, roughly speaking, it refers to women considered sexually available. The different lifeways of these four types of women are reflected in the different work done by each.

Virgins or *Teinaine*

After the relative freedom and play of childhood, a woman's first menstruation marks the arrival of preparation for adulthood and learning to work hard. Menarche, the first period, marks the ritual change from girl to woman, and the formalities of the transition are designed to prepare women for the "hard work of womanhood." At the first sign of bleeding, the girl is taken into the care of her mother and mother's sisters and confined to the house for three days. To accustom her to the "suffering of women," she is fed little in this time. She is told this will teach her how to be a selfless woman who thinks of feeding her family before herself. During this confinement she spends time with older women in her family, being told how she must behave modestly around men now that she is a young woman, how she must work hard and be responsible to the family first, and when she will bleed and how to take care of herself when she does. The details of menstruation are new to most young women, because they are told very little about sex or menstruation before this—such knowledge is thought inappropriate before they reach menarche. During the menarcheal confinement, magic incantations are said over the girl to make her beautiful, kind, and hard working. Effort is made to enhance her beauty: Her skin is rubbed with oil, her hair combed, and her stomach bound tightly to make it flat. On the third day, the woman emerges from the hut to an evening feast in the house in her honor.

Her family praises her beauty and her promise as a woman and future wife. Here is one woman's account of menarche:

> Most girls my age had already bled, even my younger sister. Everyone thought I was late, even myself, as I was more than fifteen. Everyone thought there was something wrong with me; they wanted to take me to the clinic. But, when the bleeding came, I kept it secret for a day. I knew about the feast, but I didn't know the blood would come or where it would come from. The day I first bled our whole class was out collecting coconuts. My cousin saw me when we drank coconut juice because I was sitting the wrong way. Then she went to my mother and told her. My mother came and called to me to hurry to the house. I was wrong because I was supposed to tell my family immediately. They say if you don't take care of yourself and tell your family immediately you will be like a dog. Also, once you have your period, you must be like a woman and do your work around the house. You cannot go about with boys anymore. My aunt came, and all the family came to the house. She is the one who stayed with me the whole time. She took my urine away and helped me make a menstrual cloth. It was painful because they didn't let me eat for three days. They gave me raw papaya and water and I complained. The second day they gave me pandanus and water and tied my stomach really tight with cloth to stop the pain. I said, "I'm really hungry, and I want to eat now." They told me to be a woman and not to complain. The third day they killed a pig, and all the family came; then we all had a feast. They had been eating for three days, but not me—I had been starving.

Once a woman has menstruated, she is eligible to be considered as a wife. Now she is expected to behave as a woman, which means to work hard as a woman, and this work is now centered on proving her worth as a wife. She must be obedient to family members; apply herself to housework—cooking, weaving, sweeping, and washing clothes; and do all the dullest, messiest, and most repetitive household tasks. She and her family are now responsible for the work of safe-guarding her virginity.

The Virginity Test   On the evening of her wedding in late 1990, all of Nei Teitu's* relatives begin to gather at the home of her new husband. The aunts and great-aunts arrive first, swaying under armloads of woven mats and food. They are dressed in bright colors, with large floral prints hooked around their broad hips and flower garlands encircling thick, bound hair. As they approach the house, their new in-laws call to them with warm words of greeting. The mood is festive, and laughter rings loudly. Children materialize from the gloom and converge underfoot, drawn to the excitement. They are slapped and shuffled out of the way to make space on the main house platform as guests continue to arrive.

Teitu sits methodically combing her long hair behind the blinds of a nearby house platform. This is an important night for her. Soon she will be alone with her new husband, Bakoa*, for the first time. She is a little fearful and very shy now that she knows what is about to happen. "If the man wants to hold you, you must agree," her parents told her sternly. "You must be brave and proud, as befits a married woman." Teitu knows everyone will be looking for the blood. She and her family have been very careful ever since her first menstruation to protect her virginity. She has not been alone with any men other than her cousins, she has not gone to the bush by herself to collect coconuts, and she has not walked alone between villages. She knows she is not a nikiranroro, a loose woman, and tonight the blood would show this to be true.

A uniformed brass band parades down the main road of Butaritari village during a wedding celebration. Butaritari festivities are not usually this flashy but always include much music and dance.

Bakoa's aunt had approached Teitu's family for the marriage request shortly after her nineteenth birthday. The aunt visited in the evening so no one would see her and the family would not be humiliated had the marriage request been refused. Bakoa's parents and aunt had spent several years searching for an ideal bride. As Bakoa is an oldest son, they sought a wife who was also firstborn in her family. They discussed Teitu's family at length, tracing their chiefly ties and debating their title over swamp taro pits and coconut stands. They watched Teitu from a distance at village functions to assess her manner and demeanor. Was she kind and polite? Was she humble and hard working? And, importantly, Teitu's and Bakoa's genealogies were compared to ensure they belonged to the same generation. They counted the number of generations they were separated from a common ancestor to make sure there were at least four so they were distantly enough related to properly marry.

After Bakoa's aunt visited, Teitu's parents discussed the match with her. They explained Bakoa was skillful at fishing and growing swamp taro and would feed a wife well. He seemed a kind and polite man, and his family was known in the village as generous. These are important considerations, they explained, because, when Teitu married, she would move to the home of her husband's family. Teitu wanted to honor her parents by accepting their choice. She trusted her parents' advice and had seen two older cousins married well by her aunt. Secretly, she was pleased with the match; she had seen Bakoa at gatherings at the village meeting house and liked the look of his face. After the marriage request was accepted, Bakoa had called at her home regularly with gifts of fish and toddy. She had served him food and sat near him when he visited, but until this evening they had never been alone.

As the wedding-night guests continue to gather outside the house, Teitu's mother-in-law massages her skin to a sheen with coconut oil and pats her neck with sweet powder. She helps her undress and gently lies her in a white sheet to wait for her new husband. She turns down the hanging kerosene lantern and returns to the growing, boisterous crowd outside. Teitu is left to wait. After a wave from his mother, Bakoa climbs up behind the screens into the gloom of the house platform. He smells sweet, coated in powder and *perfume. He calls to her softly. Teitu is shy of her nakedness, but she is assured by the gentleness of the way he speaks her name.*

Eventually Bakoa calls out to his mother. The mother laughs, clicks her tongue, and hurries to the couple. A shrill, gleeful wallop is heard. The mother comes rushing out with a white sheet stretched out between her hands. "A girl!" she cries. "A girl! My new daughter brings us a great honor." She raises the sheet in her outstretched arms so all the gathered relatives can see the blood. The groom's uncle touches his fingers to the stain and, with a wide, toothless grin, wipes his reddened fingers on his forehead and cheeks. He sniffs his fingers loudly and proclaims the blood to be that of a virgin. Her aunts and great aunts beam widely, tears welling in their eyes. "You have made us proud," they call, and Teitu hears their praise from within the house.

Bakoa's aunts pull a bolt of bright-red fabric from the thatched roof of the house platform. They roll out the cloth and begin trailing it around the marital hut, swathing everything in red as they go. They complete their boisterous circuit by covering themselves in the red fabric, wrapping it loosely over their clothes. They start to clown and dance for the crowd, crunching across the shell floor in their makeshift costumes.

To honor their guests, as the family of a virgin bride, the aunts start loading piles of feast foods on the house platform for their guests. The floor becomes covered in huge portions of cold foods, placed carefully on casually woven coconut fronds and huge, glossy banana leaves. The feast includes all the most special foods: fatty slabs of pork, whole-baked green sea turtle, stacks of lobster and beautiful pink-spotted reef crabs, bright-red reef fish, shiny-blue lagoon fish, and huge bowls of tuna marinated in sour toddy vinegar and tossed with coconut cream. On each mat is piled high the greatest of all prestige foods, the fibrous tubers from the giant swamp taro, cut into huge wedges and boiled and baked. Teitu's family sees the great mounds of taro, and they know Bakoa's family values the new bride and will treat her kindly and with respect. They are proud.

Women want to be virgins when they marry. If they do not bleed on their wedding night, their lives can take a sharp turn for the worse. A woman labeled in this way as a nonvirgin may well be given the cruel nickname "daughter of a dog," her marriage will be annulled, and she will be sent back to her family to be humiliated publicly and beaten privately. And with the *nikiranroro* branding, she might not receive any further marriage offers. Traditionally, women failing virginity tests on Butaritari could expect even more severe consequences. In *In the South Seas*, Robert Louis Stevenson recounts how a young bride of the king died after failing a marital virginity test. The more senior wives of the king, who at that time numbered in the dozens, were so incensed at the possibility of her having a premarital affair that they rolled her in woven mats and sat on her until she was dead. The punishment for failing the test today is not as instant and irreversible, but for the woman concerned it can be as damning. Although I was never present on a wedding evening when a test "failed," I was told of several cases where women were branded as *nikiranroro* on their wedding night because no blood was found on the mat. For example, a friend recounted the following story:

We found out this woman was a nikiranroro *because of the things that happened on her wedding night. On that day all her relatives went to the groom's house with the mats and food. There was also to be dancing, where the married couples would be sent to play with others. The relatives were all very surprised when they were about to eat the meal because they found every cup would leak. Someone had made a hole in each cup with a knife so this would happen. Then it was known that something was wrong and the family*

*was angry. Then they gave their guests pig oil, which is not good to give to anyone that
you honor. When they saw this, all the relatives ran away in ones and twos because they
were so ashamed. The bride stayed until the next morning, but she left her husband and
went home the next day when her family came to fetch her. It is her punishment to be
mocked for being a* nikiranroro. *It was all so surprising because no one knew she had sex,
except there was no blood on the wedding night. She must have had an affair before, and
no one knew about it.*

However, failing the test need not be the inevitable end of a woman's reputation.
I know of one unusual case where a strong and brave woman, then nineteen years of
age, managed to salvage her reputation and marriage with the help of a supportive
family and husband. This is her account:

*There was trouble with my family on my wedding night because there was no blood. I had
seen the blood showed at other weddings by other women who were proud of their son's
wife. There was pain but no blood. I was very surprised, because I was sure there would
be blood. After my husband and his mother checked the mat, my mother and aunt said I
can't stay with my husband because there was no blood and I might be a* nikiranroro, *and
they were ashamed. My husband's mother said to my aunts that there was one in two hundred women who were virgins but who had no blood, so I was allowed to stay with my
husband. My husband said nothing, but he was also looking for the blood. He asked me
why nothing was coming out, and I said I knew nothing. He asked me to run away with
him before my aunts came to take me away. But I refused to run away with him because I
knew I wasn't a* nikiranroro.

To the best of my knowledge, the virginity tests are never faked, in part because newly-
wed women know little of sexual matters and have no anatomical understanding of
where the blood will come from or why. Also, since most women are very protective
of their own virginity before marriage, they have little reason to suspect they will fail
the test.

Housewives or *Ainenuma*

To be a housewife is the most advantageous and socially prestigious position for
women in Butaritari society. Once married, a woman can boss her unmarried siblings, even if they are older than she. The main work of a housewife is to run the
household, see to a husband's needs, and do the "hard work" of motherhood and
birth.

Married Butaritari women are expected to obey a husband's demands. In the
first few years of marriage, they are especially acquiescent. Women become more
clever at manipulating their husbands as they grow older, but conceding to his wishes
remains a tantamount part of her contribution to the marriage. A married woman is
also expected to act with the utmost humility and discretion. She should not wander
about the village or go visiting friends without her husband's permission and should
not dress or act in a flashy manner. One woman was lambasted by public opinion for
being unnecessarily showy by "going about with bows in her hair."

Although housewives often may be under their husband's thumbs and have limits on their movements as a result, women have no reservation about wanting to have
a husband. Marriage is undeniably popular: In 1990 more than 96 percent of women
over the age of twenty-five were or had been married. Most women are married

earlier than this—the average age for a woman's first marriage is just over nineteen. Those few women who reach their late twenties and have never been married would like to marry but cannot attract husbands. Of the four women in Butaritari village over age thirty who had never had a husband, two had noticeable physical deformities, one was "simple-minded," and the fourth had a growth disorder. A main reason women find marriage so attractive is that the alternatives are much less appealing. Unmarried women are openly pitied, find themselves at the beck-and-call of all other women in the household, and have little control over their own labor.

Nikiranroro: Dishonored Women

The term *nikiranroro,* literally meaning "remnant of her generation," most inclusively refers to all women above age twenty-five or so without husbands. More specifically, *nikiranroro* women are those socially labeled as unmarried nonvirgins. They are the women in each village who signal sexual availability of some form, regardless of whether they actually are or not. This includes women who are divorced or who failed a virginity test on their wedding night. Although few in number (at most 5 percent of adult women), they are somewhat notorious in each village, at least in the sense that housewives claim "men can draw a map of all their houses." Although *nikiranroro* have the most sexual partners of any groups of women in Butaritari society, by middle-age a *nikiranroro* might have had five different sexual partners. But most partners will have been someone else's husband.

Housewives assume a superior, almost haughty, tone and stance when they meet or discuss *nikiranroro,* unless they are related to them—in which case they treat them much more kindly. They may refuse to acknowledge them at social gatherings and tend to describe them in pointedly unflattering ways. According to housewives, *nikiranroro* become such through, usually, a combination of ill fortune, lax morality, and foolish action. As one housewife stated it:

> *There are different ways a girl might become a* nikiranroro. *Mostly her parents don't care for her: They let her run around the village like a dog. Maybe some are because they had bad husbands who would hit them. There are some who were held [raped] by men in the bush and then had no choice because there would be no blood on the marriage mat. Mostly it's because they don't care for themselves.*

Whereas married women often see *nikiranroro* as fallen women, *nikiranroro* see their lives in a very different light. The words of one woman, with whom I had an open, comfortable relationship, illustrate how she chose to interpret how and why she chose to became a *nikiranroro:*

> *I separated from my husband after eight or nine months because I didn't want to marry him in the church. I didn't want to stay with him because his family were cruel and they scared me—they would fight with knives all the time. [About one year] later I loved another man and I got pregnant by him; I never told him I had his child because he was living with his family. I didn't love him so much, though, so I didn't settle down. Later about two men came and proposed to me but I refused to go with them. I want to stay a* nikiranroro, *because if I marry a man he will only use me to work. Because I am a* nikiranroro *I can go where I want and do what I want. That is better than being a wife.*

Unaine: Old Women

Old age is a time of relaxation and diminished responsibility, when a woman can expect more respect from both family and community. Old women *(unaine)* are generally classed as those over about forty-five years old, although classification as *unaine* tends to be strategic on the woman's part, rather than strictly acquired at a specific age. Once *unaine*, women no longer need do heavy work, have little direct responsibility for child care, and can spend much of their time smoking, napping, gossiping, and playing cards with friends. Older women can walk about the village without having to get their husband's approval so have more freedom to visit friends and socialize more widely. *Unaine* have more time to follow their own interests and can devote more energy to healing, midwifery, and practicing magic. These are the years when they will take the time to teach younger women these special skills.

Binabinaaine and *Binabinamane*

I Kiribati recognize that not everyone fits into these four categories of womanhood. *Binabinaaine* are biological males who adopt the look and personality of women, tying their lavalava to the side, as women do; growing their hair long and pulling it back with a comb; and taking feminine names. They also do the work of women: keeping house and minding children. *Binabinaaine* are not like other women, but they are not men either. They occupy a third gender category, a liminal state of womanhood that is often the subject of curiosity, ridicule, and teasing but is generally

An unaine, *or old woman, weaves a sleeping mat from pandanus over a plaiting board. In the background, her grandchildren laze in the heat of the afternoon.*

tolerated. They are rare, though: While I was living on Butaritari, there were no *bin-abinaaine*. When Butaritari speculate about *binabinaaine,* they most often point to a developmental origin, saying that inappropriate treatment by the parents is to blame. Maybe, they suggest, *binabinaaine* children were sons treated improperly by parents, who parted their sons' hair down the middle, were too gentle, encouraged them to do women's work, fed them too much, and made them passive like women. Maybe the parents really wanted a daughter so unknowingly channeled a son into being like a daughter, they suggest. This man-as-woman phenomenon is not unique to Kiribati: Similar "third genders" are seen in many Polynesian societies, including Tonga, Samoa, and Tahiti.

Also, a woman-as-man gender category is known on Butaritari as *binabina-mane*. Although cases throughout the chain are infrequent historically, a couple who lived in Tabonuea until recently included one partner who was a *binabinamane*. Their atypical household was the subject of considerable local attention. Here is one account of that interesting couple:

> *Nei Tabita* and Nei Biromina* lived together for many years in the same house like a man and woman. Biromina was a woman, but she dressed and acted like a man—going about with a bare chest, short hair, fishing, and collecting toddy. Biromina was even jealous just like a man and would want to fight with any men who looked at Nei Tabita. Tabita stayed in the house and was just as a housewife. Everyone teased them in the first years, but then they grew accustomed to them. Later they adopted a child. They stayed together for years, until one of them died. Now, when you see a couple of girls walking along the road hand in hand, people will call out and tease them by calling them by the names of Tabita and Biromina.*

HUSBAND AND FAMILY IN WOMEN'S LIVES

Becoming a Mother

If most *Butaritari* women want to marry, all of them want children. A woman's worth and maturity in Butaritari society is most defined by giving birth and caring for children. The first pregnancy and birth is the most treasured. The firstborn child holds a special place in any family, and it is this birth that cements the marriage in the eyes of both husband and in-laws and defines a woman as worthy and fully adult. The road to motherhood for most women begins on her wedding night, when everyone hopes she will conceive her first child.

Getting Married   "Marriage" is loosely defined in Butaritari society as a couple living together, whether or not they had a church wedding. About half of all marriages on Butaritari are arranged by the families; the rest are "love matches." But even those who leave the choice of a suitable husband to their parents can have some say in who they marry: Although many women state they did not think much of their husbands when they first saw them, they were prepared to take their parents' word that they would grow to like them. And many do. In some cases, the woman and man had seen each other in the *maneaba* and spoken, and the man then asked his family

A young mother shows off her firstborn.

to approach hers with a request for marriage. One woman, Nei Neboata, now seventy-four and an extraordinarily sharp and assertive individual, tells an atypical and romantic story of how she came to be married to her husband Tonganibeia.

> *I married a man I loved. I saw him and approached him and spoke with him because I thought he was so beautiful and so quiet. I asked him to ask for the marriage, and he agreed. When he came walking to our house in the daylight, my family asked who he was because marriage requests should be made in the night. I told them he had come for the marriage request, and they were very surprised, because it should have been his family that came, not the man. They were angry because it was not proper he had come instead of his family and because I had engineered the request myself. I argued with them, and finally they agreed because I insisted I would not marry anyone else.*

This story has a happy ending, too, because as Nei Neboata told it, she was sitting next to Tonganibeia, to whom she now has been married, happily, for fifty-four years.

Somewhat of a counterpoint to the story of Neboata and Tonganibeia is the account of a woman who had a much-less-smooth road to marriage. In this case she had a hand in accepting a betrothal and then later changed her mind in a manner her parents felt was unfair to her husband-to-be.

> *One day I was walking between two islets to visit with family, and a boy came by on a bicycle and offered me a ride. When I took a ride on his bicycle, we talked, and he asked me to marry him. I agreed because I was too* mama *[shy or ashamed] to refuse his request because I knew he was related to some of my family [by marriage]. Later his family came*

A new bride and groom return from a marriage ceremony in the Protestant church. They lead a procession down the main road to the home of the groom's family. The unhappy look on the bride's face is felt appropriate to the seriousness of the occasion: Once she left the public gaze, she beamed.

to those relatives to make the marriage request, and the two families agreed we should marry. There was a big party to celebrate on Butaritari, and then we traveled to Makin to my parents' home for the wedding. My parents were surprised I was to marry because they had not heard anything until then. We stayed at my parents' house to wait for the priest to come [on his regular visits] so we could be married. While we were at my parents' house, I spent time around the boy and got to know him better. I didn't like him. The boy had no family on Makin, so he slept in an unused hut on our land and ate with us. I was supposed to look after him, to cook his food and wash his clothes, but because I didn't like him I refused. I kept saying to my family, "Who is this man? What is he doing on our land? I have never seen him before." My parents were furious. They said I had chosen the man myself and then I had decided not to marry him. I had never seen them so angry. I told the boy to go back to Butaritari because now I didn't want him. His father even died while he stayed with us, but still he didn't leave. He just kept waiting for the priest. The date for the priest was still one month away, but my mother decided that it could not wait any more and we had to be married because he had stayed when his father died. My mother grabbed me by the hair and pushed me into a hut. She called the man to come. He pushed on my thighs so I couldn't escape. I tried to stop him but we had sex. Then it was too late.

One thing these stories show is that the woman's personality and relationship to her parents has considerable influence on who she marries and under what conditions her marriage takes place. Some couples force a parent's hand by eloping, rather than working through the formalities of marriage request, betrothal, and wedding. In most cases the family accepts the liaison, and the marriage endures. The marriage is considered cemented when the woman loses her virginity. Usually the elopement is to the boy's family, who will celebrate the union for three days and then gather the family and take the couple to the bride's parents to announce the *fait accompli* and, they hope, to continue the celebrations.

Giving Birth   Soon after the wedding or elopement, the families of both newly-weds will anticipate a pregnancy. The mother-in-law is particularly vigilant in keeping an eye on the bride. If the bride stops menstruating and starts feeling nauseated, she will often confide in her mother-in-law that she suspects she is pregnant. Even though it is considered important to keep an impending birth secret for as long as possible, especially to protect the mother-to-be from mischievous spirits or malevolent magic, the mother-in-law generally has a difficult time hiding her pride and joy. Although she does not exactly break the secret, she can drop hints that help others guess the truth. She may announce she is off to collect fat, juicy crabs to put on the fire because her daughter-in-law has a craving for them. As soon as she is known to be pregnant, the mother-to-be is treated with tender concern. She is dissuaded from doing hard work and returns to the home of her mother at mid-pregnancy in preparation for the birth.

Pregnancy is considered a time of particular vulnerability for both mother and unborn child. The mischief of spirits must be guarded against by the mother's staying around the house as much as possible, and she should be surrounded by as much calm and beauty as possible at all times. If the mother is surrounded by beautiful things and eating beautiful foods, it is said, the baby will be beautiful, feeling the happiness of the mother. This form of "sympathetic" magic is common in Butaritari society, where like induces like. The mother is encouraged to bathe facing the sunrise and sunset. She is hindered from eating "ugly" foods such as the porpoise, which has bad teeth, or flat fish with both eyes on one side of the body, which may result in a cross-eyed child. Instead, she eats piles of pink-spotted reef crabs, which will give the child glowing cheeks. Care is taken to have the mother sit and eat with attractive people—those with straight, white teeth; pale skin; and thick hair—and avoid the less-attractive or unfortunate (such as infertile women). (I was fortunate enough that by Butaritari standards I was considered attractive, if a little skinny, and pregnant women were, at the very least, comfortable to sit near me. I can only speculate that interviewing would have been much more difficult if I had been considered plainer, because I could have been unwelcome in the company of pregnant women.)

Beginning in the seventh month of pregnancy, the mother is given specially prepared herbal drinks to encourage a safe and rapid labor. The midwife will visit and massage her abdomen, and she will be forced to rest from any physical labor. In the final stages of the pregnancy, the woman is placed in the care of her female relatives and the deliverer. Husbands are excluded from watching or participating in the birth. Women say this is the rule for two reasons. First, birth is very painful, and they do not want their husbands to see them cry or complain. Second, as one woman stated it,

> *It is possible that my husband would like to be there for the birth. But I don't want him there because, after all, the pain is all his fault. If he came near I would shout to him that he was to blame and he can get lost until the pain is over.*

A Birth   It was shortly after sunset when Nei Tekima* felt the contractions of birth coming more quickly. She called to her mother, who was sitting in the kitchen hut carefully chopping tobacco with the kitchen knife for her evening cigarette. Nei Tekima's mother knows much about birth, having mothered nine children and buried two more in infancy. Nei Tekima had moved from the house of her husband's family two months before so she could be close to her mother for the birth of her first child. Tekima's mother sharply called her sister's daughter to her side. "Go and collect your great aunt for the delivery," she orders her. "Tell her I will soon be a grandmother."

Tekima's mother and oldest sister gather her up and help her climb onto the house platform. As a kerosene lantern is hooked under the sharp roof of the house, a rat scurries into the dark corner of the thick pandanus thatch. A crowd of young children silently materializes out of the gloom, drawn to the sudden activity. The women wave them away and release woven screens down over the open sides of the house. Wide, brown eyes and coy smiles can be seen peeping through the edges of the screens. Tekima's sister shoos them away with a harsh word and a sharp swing of her hand and proceeds to hang sheets to fill any gaps. Once Tekima is settled, Tekima's mother encourages her to drink several cups of juice from the kiaou fruit mixed with rainwater. She explains the slippery juice will hasten labor, making both baby and placenta slip out easily.

As the contractions increase, Tekima's aunt arrives to direct the delivery. She was taught the skills of the midwife by her own aunt as a special inheritance. Tekima's youngest sister ambles across the coral yard of the compound and lightly places a plastic bowl of well water and a piece of soap on the platform edge. After carefully washing her hands, the aunt climbs onto the platform, settles herself beside Tekima, and places her hands across Tekima's abdomen. After carefully feeling the baby's position, she ties an old but clean lavalava under Nei Tekima's breasts and pulls it taut. She explains this will ease the pain and show the baby the way out—so it cannot retreat back into the body. Tekima's sister keeps the flies from her sweaty skin and cools her by fanning her face and body in a slow, rhythmic motion. Her mother massages her lower back and speaks reassuringly in her ear.

As the contractions come faster, Tekima stays as quiet as she can be, gritting her teeth and holding onto her sister. The most important part of the birth, Nei Tekima knows, is the pain. It is the pain, her mother has told her, that makes the child come out. The pain is necessary—a birth without pain is not a real birth. But the pain causes her to cry out. Her aunt grasps her hand tightly and chastens her sternly. "You must not complain, Tekima; you must behave as befits a brave woman. This is good pain; it is the pain of birth. Soon you will be a mother."

Tekima leans back against her mother while her aunt guides out the baby. "A girl!" cries the aunt, with obvious delight. Tekima is surprised, since in all her talks with her mother-in-law she had been led to believe it would be a son. She has heard sons tend to sit to the right of the abdomen in pregnancy, as this baby did. Although she suspects her husband may secretly have wished for a son, she knows he will be happy for her that she has her daughter. She knows a daughter will be able to help her in the house and will be of great comfort in her older years.

Tekima's mother calls out the news of the birth to the new father, who has been waiting with his wife's male relatives within calling distance on a platform at the other side of the household compound. Within seconds the news of the birth begins to travel through the village. It is especially important news because this is Tekima's first birth. Now she and her husband, as new parents, will gain a greater respect in the village than they had as a childless couple. They are both now fully adult.

Tekima's mother moves to help with the delivery of the placenta. It is delivered quickly and easily. Her mother massages her abdomen to ensure the placenta has been completely expelled, checks to make sure it is whole and none is left inside, and then places the placenta in a plastic basin. It will not be burned, because she knows this will give the child a red skin rash. Rather, it will be buried carefully with a germinated co-conut over the top. Later Tekima's daughter will be able to point to that coconut tree as a sign of the importance of her birth to her family.

After the placenta is delivered, Tekima's grandmother is called to cut the umbilical cord. She measures three fingers down from the baby's body, massaging back the blood toward the baby. She takes a weaving board and rubs the cord up and down until it be-comes soft and pliable and ties a section with cotton. As she works she speaks secret words under her breath. These powerful words will make the baby grow into a brave, beautiful, and hard-working woman. Tekima's husband's toddy knife is used to cut the cord. The knife is not cleaned specially in preparation for the cutting, but this is a special knife. In everyday use it is reserved for scratching the coconut-flower spathe when tap-ping toddy.

While the cord is being cut, the midwife pulls a clean, flowered cloth over the sole of her bare foot and uses her stretched leg to push up between Tekima's legs. The aunt ex-plains this is to return the external sex organs back into place, so she will not have health problems later. She then performs a short, gentle massage on Tekima's abdomen and back to move the internal organs back into their correct alignment. About a month from now, Tekima will have her stomach bound to finish the process of returning everything to its correct place. During this time, the aunt reminds her mother, Tekima will have to avoid physical work and rest so the organs will not be pulled out of place again.

The baby, now touched by the grandmother's magic, is placed on a finely woven pandanus-leaf mat. Tekima's sister passes her a special drink from the uri *bush, which is said to stop bleeding after birth. As soon as Tekima feels able to move, her sisters help her to the wash hut located near the well at the edge of the compound. The cool water is soothing relief. Birth and pregnancy, her grandmother has kept reminding her, makes a woman's body hot and unhealthy. Like all new mothers, Tekima is encouraged to bathe in cool water and lie in breezes so her body will cool and her breast milk will be healthy, rich, and plentiful.*

After Tekima is settled again, her smiling husband brings her a small meal of rice and coconut, washed down with coconut toddy mixed with coconut milk. Tekima's grand-mother has overseen the meal preparation, trying to choose the foods known to produce the best breast milk.

As the clear and humid morning progresses, a stream of laughing members of the husband's family begins arriving at the house to admire the new child. They are carrying gifts of fabric, mats, and food. They sit on the main house platform, sipping kabubu, *a drink of dried pandanus fruit and prepared specially for the occasion. This time is called the "reddening," when the family sits by the fire and celebrates the birth. Tekima dozes beside her new child under a mosquito net across the compound. The proud, new grand-mother sits stretched out along the edge of the platform, protectively fanning cool air onto Tekima and the baby with a wide pandanus-leaf fan with one hand and shooing off chickens with the other.*

The Butaritari think of themselves as being specially knowledgeable about giv-ing birth. This is reflected in the story of the explorer Te Raka from Butaritari, who taught the Nauruans (or in other versions, people on other Tungaru islands) how to give birth.

This is a true story but a very, very old story. The fisherman Te Raka from Butaritari taught the people in Nauru how to give birth. They were ignorant before then. Two women called Nei Korokua and Nei Koromaete would see to all the births on Nauru. If the mother was about to give birth, they would cut open her stomach to take out the baby, and the mother would die. They would chant "Let the baby live, and let the mother die." A princess on Nauru lived alone on a point on the island. She was kept there because her father didn't want her to marry because then she would get pregnant and die. Of course, she had no mother because she had died when she gave birth. Then Te Raka arrived, flying with the feathers of a bird so big it could lift canoes. The princess found him near her house, and he stayed there, and she thought he was a bird. But at night he came out as Te Raka and would sleep with her. When she got pregnant, Te Raka showed himself. When she was ready to give birth, everyone waited for her to die. But she had Te Raka's help, and then everyone was amazed because she had her child and she wasn't dead. Everyone wondered where the child had come from. The relatives looked all over her body and couldn't see the door where the child came from. When they found it, they killed those two women who would cut the stomachs open.

Being a New Mother

Women put the child to the breast as soon as possible after a birth and always by the third day. Virtually all women breastfeed—more than 98 percent in my samples— unless the breast is dry or infected or the child cannot suckle, for example, because it has a harelip. Breastfeeding is thought of as best for the baby, and women go to great lengths to keep breast milk healthy and copious.

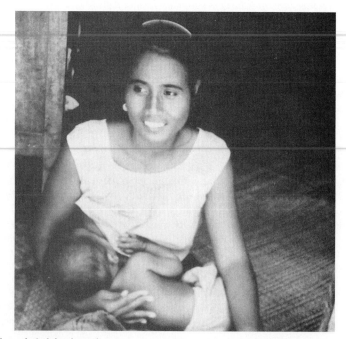

All women breastfeed if they have the opportunity to do so.

Any external or internal heating in the woman is thought to reduce the quantity of breast milk because it dries it up or makes it "spoil." Lactating women keep out of the sunlight as much as possible, especially in the first few months after birth. When they do go out, they always cover their breasts with a thick towel or lavalava to keep off the sun. Every effort is made to avoid the heat of the cooking fire, so new mothers rarely cook. The new mother is careful to bathe in cool water and sit in cool breezes. She also avoids all salty foods, especially salted, dried fish, because salt in food is thought to make breast milk salty, so the child will fuss on the breast.

Butaritari custom states couples should avoid sex after a birth for as long as a mother is breastfeeding, which is usually around twelve months. Male semen is thought to be a strong fluid that can taint the woman's breast milk and make the child sick. Symptoms of such illness in the child include diarrhea, vomiting, and malaise, and a child sickened in this way is said to develop more slowly than its peers. Many couples, however, fail to ascribe to the abstinence belief. More than one-third of couples reported that at some point they had sex soon after the birth. In doing this, they say, the child will be introduced to the semen-enriched milk soon after it is put to the breast and will be accustomed to it from the outset. In this way, the sickness associated with changing from the weaker to stronger breast milk is said to be avoided. This does not mean couples immediately return to regular sex after birth; rather, they may have sex once after birth and then may wait a few months to begin more regular activity. Some couples are forced by parents to sleep separately after a birth, at least for the first two to three months. Couples living neolocally or separately from parents, away from the keen eye and sharp tongue of a mother, start having sex sooner after a birth. So, regarding traditional restrictions on sex while breastfeeding, the experience of couples addresses but does not necessarily reflect the ideology—unless mothers-in-law have the opportunity to preach what they themselves do not always practice.

Being a Wife

A new marriage will be strengthened with the birth of a child, and women who fail to have any children may find themselves unappreciated by their husbands and in-laws and contending with the possibility of separation and divorce. Some couples, like Neboata and Tonganibeia, are deeply devoted to each other, have great respect for each other, and are mutually supportive. This is the marital situation to which women always hope an arranged marriage will lead. This mutual respect and caring approximates closely what Butaritari women describe as the best sort of love for husbands.

Marriage and Love   For many women, what they describe as love comes after marriage rather than before. The words of Nei Betiraoi*, age fifty-three, illustrate how a woman may come to love a husband:

> My husband and I didn't love each other in the beginning. As is the custom, my husband's aunt came to request our marriage from my family. I didn't want to get married then, and I didn't want to marry him. But my family did not listen to my words. They said I should marry him because he was a hard worker and because we are in the same generation.

After we married, I began to love him because I was ashamed not to. Before we were married and when we first married, I hated him in my heart but I was careful not to let him see my hate. But he knew I didn't love him because I would speak sharply to him for no reason. It was about one month after we married that I began to love him. Maybe this is because the sex stopped hurting, and he was kind, and because I had no choice. He was a good man, always working hard and helpful. When I am busy with the baby, he will do all the washing and help me with the chores. He is a good man.

In this way love is discussed less as an overwhelming emotion and more as something that develops expectantly out of obligation to the marriage by both partners, something people who behave well toward their parents deserve. It is shaming for a woman not to love a husband who treats her well. It is a source of enormous pride for both husbands and wives to be seen to be loving to their partners—a woman who fails to love a husband who is helpful, hard working, and kind is held in very low regard by family and friends. This is very different from the Western image of conjugal love, which focuses on an idealized and romantic bond.

A sense of fatalism is also associated with the development of Butaritari marital love. Once their virginity is lost, women accept the finality of the marriage and— even if they had marked reservations about their partner—the need to get on with the work of acting like wives, which includes loving their husbands. Also, many women who resisted marriage before were happily surprised once they began having sex. I have yet to meet a married Butaritari woman who complained about her husband's qualities as a lover.

Marriage and Sex   Sexual access is central to the marital relationship. Women reiterate that it is vital to give a husband as much sex as he wants, whenever he asks for it. To deny a husband sex is against the woman's best interests, they argue, because it will press him to seek out *nikiranroro*. On the other hand, women should never initiate sex. All overtures need to come from the husband; therefore, he controls how often and when they have sex. A woman perceived as sexually assertive within a marriage delivers a negative and threatening message to the husband—that is, that the woman may be behaving in a similar manner with other men. With all this, married women take a passive role in outlining the sexual activity that occurs in a marriage. They do, however, have some control at specific times—during menstruation, in advanced pregnancy, after birth, and during notable sickness—by discouraging their husbands from having sex with them. Their arguments are gauged in selfless terms—for example, it would damage the unborn baby's head at advanced stages of pregnancy, the husband will become ill if they have sex during menstruation, the child will become sick while breastfeeding, and so on. It is almost inconceivable that a Butaritari wife would refuse her husband sex just because she was not in the mood.

While women think they should be sexually available to their husbands, men do not want their wives to be wanting either. It is humiliating to a man to have an unsatisfied spouse, and as women report it, men make special efforts to please their wives. A satisfied wife is thought to be a sign of a loving marriage. Women say husbands are concerned about their wives' "needs" because if the women were unhappy, they might think of being with another man who would do "better things" for them.

This idea that sexual satisfaction is essential to both partners in order for the integrity of the marriage to be maintained was a clear theme in interviews. Regular intercourse is expected and provided—by both sexes—through the reproductive years. So, married Butaritari have lots of sex. Sex is, at the very least, a daily activity between the wedding and the first pregnancy, and sex remains a common activity through years of marriage and up until the woman enters menopause. Even married women who had at least three children and had been married more than ten years reported having sex at least once a week, and the majority had sex at least three to four times a week. The decline in sexual interest and sexual activity is precipitous after women enter the ages of *unaine,* though. What became most apparent in interviews is that husbands tended to "stop thinking about sex" only after women had gone through menopause. This is also the age at which women become the village sexual jokers and start to act in a gregarious, rowdy, and explicit manner at celebrations.

Sex in marriage is mainly a nighttime activity and takes place after other household members are sleeping. In a village of open-sided huts, the men's maxim is "a quiet wife is a good wife." Couples may seek privacy from in-laws and children by going to the beach or abandoned huts.

Fellatio is uncommon and reportedly never practiced by older couples. This is because women say the penis "smells bad" and because they claim to be "ignorant" of how to do it in Butaritari. They appreciate that, although it may be enjoyable for men, men did not want them to practice fellatio if they themselves did not wish to do so. The appropriateness of female sexual passivity does not prevent men from being concerned about women enjoying sex (in fact, quite the opposite), but in some senses the act of fellatio would seem (on both sides) as if the woman were taking too much initiative in the sex act—and could, therefore, also do the same with a man other than her husband. Cunnilingus is a different matter. Men are concerned about women, particularly their wives, enjoying sex both because it is an intimate and pleasant thing in marriage to take efforts to please a wife and because it will "stop her thinking of other men." Ultimately, women believe men practice cunnilingus only for their own pleasure and pride, rather than for that of the women.

This is an abbreviated version of the story surrounding the "invention" of cunnilingus in Tungaru, which explains this aspect of "male pride."

It comes from the games King (Tem) Binoka [ruled 1878–92] invented for his amusement on Abemama Atoll. Binoka, a powerful man with many wives and a ruthless disposition, would take his pick of all virgins on the three islands under his control. He married all the prettiest and raped and returned the rest. Binoka had a special swimming pool that he would surround with a fence of his naked, kneeling wives. Binoka had a special predilection for the smell of female genitalia and would not let his wives wash often. It was with his female fence that Binoka invented "his game." He later taught his "trick" to his three sons, and this is why today men from Abemama are considered those with the greatest skill in this area of sexual activity. It is important to note that, following Binoka's example, although it is appreciated that women may enjoy the "game," that men do it because they enjoy the act and because they are proud and want to show their skill. For this reason it is said that Binoka and his sons also would practice their skill on old women, which proved their skill was consummate regardless of how sexually attractive the woman was, and they could thus be very proud of their prowess. Today Abemama women are said to be the country's experts at fellatio as well.

Nikiranroro *and Lust*   Butaritari women make a distinction between lust and marital love. Lust is a sexual emotion men feel for *nikiranroro;* love is for their wives. This distinction is fairly cut-and-dried, and any relationship between a man and a *nikiranroro* is expected to be based solely on her physical attractiveness. If women tolerate a husband's wandering from the marital mat, as they often do ("I'd absolutely rather he went to her than came home when he's been drinking"), they expect the sex with a *nikiranroro* will be absolutely directed only at the man's sexual enjoyment. A wife will only feel particularly threatened by a *nikiranroro's* sexuality if she discovers her husband is showing sexual concern for the woman. Satisfying another woman is a breach of loyalty to the wife. However, as *nikiranroro* are thought to have magical skills to lure and trap men, the men are often not the first to be blamed for the transgression of being captivated enough to want to please a *nikiranroro*. If the man appears "tricked" into going back repeatedly to the *nikiranroro,* a wife may be prepared to fight the *nikiranroro* for her husband, as the following story illustrates:

> *A woman discovered from word of mouth that her husband had been having an affair with a* nikiranroro *for some time. Her husband was away, and she went to the store where the* nikiranroro *worked to confront her. She went straight up to her, looked her in the eye, and asked her if it were true. The* nikiranroro *admitted the affair but told the wife that she had not tempted the husband; rather, the husband had initiated the sex. The wife told the woman she was a* kameaka *[nymphomaniac/dog] and did nothing except lie around with men. The* nikiranroro *replied the woman was* koko *[jealous] because the husband loved her better. She said she knew this to be true because the husband kept coming to her and giving her oral sex. She said she was better in bed than the wife because the husband had told her so. And, if the husband loved her better, then he wouldn't come to a* nikiranroro. *At this point the wife exploded and called the* nikiranroro *outside. They began to fight furiously with their hands. The woman ripped off the* nikiranroro's *shirt and began to hit her around the face.*

Extramarital Sex   The Butaritari display a clear double standard toward both the expectation and treatment of men's and women's extramarital sexual activity. Whereas male adultery is almost expected and often implicitly tolerated by women—and encouraged by other men—female adultery is reportedly rare and seldom tolerated. Adultery itself is loosely defined, and may extend to a man catching an accidental glimpse of a naked, married woman or whistling to her when he passes. Married women, so often under the watchful eyes of husbands and families, have almost no opportunity for marital infidelity. Further, the social sanctions against straying are so severe that women feel a strong disincentive to even let the slightest hint of impropriety develop. A woman suspected of infidelity could expect, at the very least, a severe beating, possibly to be shamefully divorced, and, in extreme cases, to be killed by her angry husband.

Because of lack of inclination and opportunity, female adultery is said by Butaritari women to occur hardly ever. If it did, discretion would be essential. In all cases, the man accused of having an affair with a married woman is considered to be acting out of hate or revenge for her husband—committing a crime against the husband's property, not just conducting the affair for pleasure. In this way it seems that, for men, adultery is a brave and dangerous act, and I suspect it rarely goes undiscovered when it happens; that is, details of a brave and daring act are very likely to be recounted. On the other hand, I get no sense from the women with whom I spoke that they thought of the possibility of adultery as sexually exciting or as revenge against their husbands. Of course, given the punishments involved, women would be understandably reluctant to admit any extramarital activity. Even bearing this in mind, I retain the impression that they did not generally seek or wish to accept any sexual partners other than their husbands, and for this reason few are probably having extramarital intercourse—at least, less often than men claim to.

Courtesy Sexual Relations

Three special courtesy or customary forms of sexual relationship may take place on Butaritari. *Te tinaba* is a courtesy sexual relationship, with socially specified rights, that is more common in the southern atolls of Tungaru than in the north. It may be contracted between a man's wife and his classifactory uncle. (Classifactory relatives share a social rather than a biological bond.) This relationship is said to be allowed only if the wife agrees; however, a wife is expected to always agree to such arrangements—to not do so would be considered clearly disobeying her husband's family. In return for providing the man with sexual intimacy and special kindness, the woman expects to be conferred property rights at some later time. The *tinaba* involving sex is reportedly very rare on Butaritari, although passing gossip tells of *tinaba*-style relationships based on special care and kindness—but not involving sexual access—sometimes developing.

More common on Butaritari is a special in-law sexual relationship, *te eiriki,* which—unlike *te tinaba*—does not transcend generation lines. Classifactory in-laws in the same generation may have sexual access to each other on a short-term basis. These affinal categories are considered to be ideal remarriage partners and were also men's traditional concubines in the polygynous system. The *eiriki* arrangement is not analogous to the *tinaba* in the sense that it is not a reciprocal-obligatory relationship but is classified as simply a "game" or entertainment. Married women said they do not particularly like such games, but they feel powerless to resist them because to do so would show their "weakness." As one older woman put it:

> If my female cousin comes to me and says "don't look for your husband tonight, because he is coming home to stay with me," I feel I should go along with it. If I don't agree, then I will be ashamed because it means I have no bravery. If I really respect the custom, I would even encourage my husband to go to her, to show how I am brave to stay with the custom. Otherwise my cousin may say I am jealous of her. After that time my cousin will be my first enemy, though, even if I am the only one who knows it. I would be proud because she had to use the custom to get my husband, and she is shamed.

On Butaritari it is a stated tradition for festive, casual sexual play to occur between two families celebrating a wedding. On the night of the wedding, the two sides of the family, in happiness and pride for the couple, will hold a large feast and drinking session. *Te kanobutika* is a special dance, where the married members of the two families line up on two sides, pair off, and then retreat into the dark. Although in decades past this resulted in casual sexual intercourse, interviewed women stated they felt this was now inappropriate for married women; instead, it was much better to just "let the man touch your skin and to only have a game."

VIOLENCE IN WOMEN'S LIVES

Angry Men and Brave Women

While women may, often out of a strong sense of loyalty, propriety, and obligation, grow to feel what they term love for their husbands, marriage can be a violent place for them. Wife beating is arguably the most common form of violence in Butaritari society. In comparison, domestic violence against children or parents is strikingly rare and carries strong social sanction. Neighbors and family will intervene quickly if a child is being hit harder or with more anger than punishing misbehavior would warrant. On the other hand, low-grade, angry violence by a husband toward a wife is not only tolerated but also implicitly expected, even by a wife. Women told me on many occasions that their husbands were "not ashamed" to hit them and that it is expected if, for example, after a full day's fishing or farming, a husband comes home to a wife gossiping with friends who has not prepared his dinner. Because wives are expected to assent to their husband's wishes, husbands are given leeway to encourage "wifely" behavior with a strike. This form of physical reprimand is a common and accepted part of gender relations in many nonindustrial (and industrial) societies (Brown 1992). Wives generally accept the odd cuff as part of the deal of marriage, particularly when they are wasteful or lax around the house. For example, in the following case, the woman herself and her friends agreed she was probably "asking for it":

> My husband only ever hit me really hard once. That was when we first settled down. It was because I burnt the coconut leaves we were to use for thatch. I set them on fire because my husband kept saying he would soak them in water so they would open so I could weave them. Eventually I just got tired of waiting and decided to let him know I wasn't going to wait any longer.

And, in retrospect, the woman felt the defiance of her act was worth the beating.

Sometimes, particularly after a sour-toddy drinking session, violence toward wives escalates into a severe bashing. The ubiquity of "black eyes" on housewives is testament to it being common. Of the twenty-three women I interviewed in depth about the nature of their marriages, eight reported what could be classified as severe beatings. In all but one of these cases, the husband was a drinker and prone to fits of *koko* jealousy. Certainly, at night, amid open-sided huts, unfolding domestic fights were hard to miss, as the following extract from my journal shows:

> Last night was a very bad night. Burea* spent yesterday drinking toddy [with male friends] and came back to the house in a drunk, aggressive mood. Just as I was dropping

off to sleep, Nei Tabera* and Burea [her husband] started to argue. She started by telling him off for spending all the money on sour toddy, and he fairly promptly finished the argument with what sounded like several cracks of his fist. I could hear surprised, muffled cries from Tabera—she was obviously trying not to cry out. Things were quiet after that. I lay awake for some time in frustrated anger. I didn't know if things were quiet because Tabera was knocked out or because Burea had won the disagreement. Eventually, the baby started whimpering, and I could hear Tabera getting up and dealing with him, and then I managed to sleep at last. I felt so absolutely helpless. When I came out this morning, Tabera was sitting in front of the house doing laundry. She had a couple of nasty bruises on her upper arm and what appeared to be a blackened eye. She smiled and rolled her eyes when she saw me come out, indicating—as I read it—that she knew that I knew but didn't want to discuss it. I sat by her and chatted for a few minutes. I am still having trouble grappling emotionally with the sense of women's resignation toward violence, although I understand intellectually that, as someone mentioned the other day, there is no point in trying to ask a man to stop because it would only make things worse once a man was in a hitting way. (Field Journal, January 25, 1991)

Later, Tabera was sent to the hospital on Tarawa in the advanced stages of pregnancy when she began heavy vaginal bleeding after being hit by her husband when he was *koko*.

Once violence becomes brutal, a wife is able to draw on friends and family, especially her brother, for help and physical protection. When women start to fear for their lives, they will grab the children and run and hide anywhere they can—in *babai* pits, in the bush. If a woman runs to her family, she must be able to convince them she is not to "blame"—that despite irreproachable behavior on her part, her husband has become cruel. If she can convince her family to provide protection, the woman has the upper hand. The husband is forced to shame himself by visiting the family and begging the wife to return home. On such occasions the man feels the sting of his in-laws, who will jeer and tease him for having to beg so pathetically to have his wife back.

Many women feel to return violence with violence is dangerous, but women admire wives who hit back, considering it an act of bravery and justifiable defiance. However, few women hit back. The message would be clear: She wishes he were dead. A characteristic revenge of a brave woman against a violent husband is to wait until he is asleep, then squeeze and yank on his testicles. The Butaritari view of male anatomy draws the testicles as connected to a central organ by a thin cord. If the cord is torn, they say, the man will die. Thus, pulling on the testicles is tantamount to an attempt on the man's life. This is well-illustrated in the following story, here given secondhand:

This woman was in the maneaba *playing bingo when her husband arrived in a very angry mood. He had been waiting at home for a meal and had decided to go out and find her. He grabbed her by the hair and began to hit her in front of the crowd at the* maneaba. *All the time he was telling her she was a bad woman and she should have seen to the house first. Two men jumped up and grabbed the husband's arms. The wife, seizing the opportunity, kicked him squarely in the groin. The husband collapsed and was having trouble even breathing. The wife started crying and trying to comfort her husband, assuring him between sobs that she didn't want to kill him. For some time after that, the man was named in the village as "the man whose wife tried to kill him in the* maneaba."

Whereas men can use physical violence to express anger or dissatisfaction, women have other means to channel strong conjugal emotions. Butaritari women are often quick to use sharp words, and many have a biting verbal repertoire when they choose to use it—which can be often. More tragically, some women turn their frustration, anger, and hurt inward, and suicide or suicide attempts emerge as the ultimate expression of their emotion.

In looking at death records for Butaritari, I have estimated the frequency of suicide on the island but with less-than-satisfying results, so I cannot accurately gauge how common it is as a cause of death. I came across written or verbal accounts of five women's suicides (and one of a man) over the previous fifty years. In addition, three out of the twenty-three women I interviewed in depth about their lives admitted to attempted suicides. For all these attempts, the women cited unhappy marriages as their motive.

The common means for women attempting suicide is to hang themselves from a tree. Often this is done in a place where someone is likely to come by, such as on a pathway. If discovered before the act is completed, the suicide attempt can send a powerful message to a spouse, as the following account by a woman about two decades after a suicide attempt shows:

> *My husband is a good man now. He works hard, and he doesn't fight with me. He's not* koko *(jealous) now, even if he was in his younger days. When we married, he was a bad man, not talking to me and drinking too much. I always obeyed him, only doing what he wanted me to do and not going to gatherings. I was* koko *too, but only on one occasion. After we were married, we went to [her home island to the south], and they threw a party for us in the* maneaba. *All my aunts and cousins came and played games with my husband. I didn't like those sort of [flirty] games. I was ashamed of the way they played. I wanted to kill myself. I went off secretly to a house and tried to tie a lavalava around my neck. My husband found me and stopped me. He promised not to play that way with my cousins any more if I was so* koko.

In this vein, suicide or an attempt at suicide is a culturally recognized means for a woman to shift her shame to the person who is causing her anger or pain. Had this woman been successful, as she may have been if her husband had not intervened, her shame would have become the shame of her husband and cousins for flirting and making her *koko*.

Inasmuch as suicide is driven by or associated with intense emotion it is also sometimes interpreted as the act of the temporarily insane, in that insanity is derived from magic or intense emotion. Most often that intense emotion is the jealous anger of *koko*—the reason given in all of the women's successful and attempted suicides for which I have records.

"Koko Is a Murdering Thing*"*   The most dangerous emotion in Butaritari is the sexual jealousy of one spouse over another—the fierce and feared emotional complex of *koko*. Whereas *koko* in a partner is taken as a signal of love and commitment, particularly since a married man is never *koko* of his girlfriend—only his wife—it is also at the core of much of the violence by men in Butaritari society. As one woman put it, *"Koko* is a murdering thing."

TABLE 2-1   VIOLENCE IN MARRIAGES IN RELATION TO A HUSBAND'S CHARACTER

Husband's Character	Excessively Violent	Not Excessively Violent
Heavy drinker/*koko*	7	0
Heavy drinker/not *koko*	0	5
Not a drinker/*koko*	1	3
Not a drinker/not *koko*	0	7
Total	8	15

Violence in marriages in relation to a husband's character, according to the self-reports of twenty-three wives.

When a man suddenly feels *koko,* violence is expected (see Table 2-1). It is a volatile and dangerous emotion, considered almost impossible to control. Women say men are either inclined to *koko* or not—some husbands never show it; others show it all the time, despite having no socially legitimate reason to do so. The legitimate reasons for a man to exhibit *koko* is if he is aware of a hint or suggestion of another man having any form of intimate connection with his wife. This may be as minor as him suspecting she is looking at, or even thinking of, another man. If any clues or evidence of a wife having an affair with another man emerge, *koko* can become a murdering passion.

A damaging manifestation of *koko* is nose biting. By ripping off the tip of his wife's nose with his teeth, the husband not only destroys his wife's looks but also leaves her with a permanent and public signal of his *koko.* Although Butaritari are usually very quick to laugh at and tease anyone with a physical disability, they do not do this with women who have had their noses bitten off. I heard one mother chide a small child, "Don't laugh at the woman because it's not like she was born with no nose. She has none because her husband loves her so much." Nose biting has become less visible in the last few years, particularly since the regular visits of Australian plastic-surgery teams to Tarawa allow lost noses to be reconstructed. Medical staff at the hospital in Tarawa see ten to fifteen cases of bitten noses in the country each year.

But men not only turn the emotion of *koko* outward into defacing wives but also inward into self-mutilation. A common sign of *koko* distress in men is drawing a knife heavily across the top of the forearm. The scars that remain serve as a constant reminder to the wife of the pain she caused him.

As shown in the last story, *koko* emotion is not confined to men. Butaritari women tend to more often internalize the emotion of *koko,* and it manifests as sadness and despair. This explains why *koko* is cited as a cause of female suicide more often than for male suicide. Not all women turn their emotions inward, though, and aggrieved wives can be as violent as their husbands. However, a main difference is that they tend to turn to violence toward other women rather than toward their spouses. Women are also less likely to fight on the mere suggestion of adultery and more likely to wait for proof before confronting the girlfriend. Most physical fights between women are *koko*-based, when an aggrieved wife calls out to the *nikiranroro* to face her charges and her fury, usually in front of a gathering crowd. Although the *buto,* a small, sharp stick that kills by being driven behind the clavicle or into the mouth, is considered the weapon of choice, most often the household knife is the weapon of convenience. I failed to unearth any examples of a woman dying in one of these fights on Butaritari, although they did turn up in High Court transcripts from other islands in the chain. However, the fear of a furious wife is sufficient so *niki-ranroro* having affairs with married men note the need for constant vigilance to watch out for angry wives.

Because *koko* is considered such a powerful and uncontrollable emotion, it is also a forgivable one. This is illustrated in the following story, where the perpetrator is ultimately excused from murder by the victim's family on the basis of *koko* insanity:

> One man, consumed with koko, was so scared by the idea of his wife looking at other men that he never wanted to let his wife out of his sight. While she wove mats in their house, he would insist she look directly ahead at the cupboard at the back of the house and would not allow her to look sideways as she worked, in case a man was passing by the house. Sometimes his koko would become so strong that he would tie her feet to the house post when he left the house, sometimes returning and keeping her trussed for a day or two at a time, during which he would feed her by hand and see to her needs. He often beat her, either in the house with the screens down, or he would take her to the bush and beat her with impunity where no one could see. Eventually, the wife died in the midst of one of these battering sessions—hit on the side of the head with a tobacco box. The man was never socially considered a "murderer" but, rather, to have been so consumed by his love for his wife that he had become insane. After the wife died, her family, feeling pity for him now he was alone, gave him the wife's younger (half) sister as a new wife. At the time of the remarriage, the new wife and her mother secretly practiced magic to reduce the man's koko. The man is said to have been an exemplary spouse to the new wife, showing no overt signs of koko, providing toddy and fish regularly, and not beating his wife.

This story also mentions one way *koko* can be controlled—through magic. Most often this involves use of magical words and incantations. Sometimes, if it seems a husband is about to explode in *koko,* a wife with special magical knowledge will spit in her hand and say a few special words under her breath in the hope it will calm him.

Although it is dangerous and violent, both men and women see *koko* as an expression of conjugal love. For this reason, it is treated with the greatest respect. It is also a very powerful regulator of female sexuality within marriage. Being such a volatile emotion, *koko* needs to be heeded and treated seriously by a wife. The threat of a lost nose or life is generally sufficient to keep wives away from other men.

Sex and Violence   It is not only married women who are exposed to male violence but also unmarried women. Sexual coercion of unmarried women is not rare in Butaritari, although it is impossible to accurately estimate how common it is. As is the case in American society, definitions of what constitutes sexual violence or coercion vary markedly, particularly between men and women and especially between coerced women and their attackers. My (feminist) working definition is that I count as sexual violence any incident where the woman involved considers it was coerced.

The Butaritari distinguish two forms of sexual coercion. *Kawakawa,* or crawling, involves a young man sneaking into houses at night while a woman sleeps to "steal a touch" (married women sleep without undergarments). These episodes are most often buoyed by sour toddy and the urging of a young man's male friends to show his daring. This is similar to the "night crawling" described of many Polynesian societies, including by Margaret Mead in Samoa. Trying to get into a house and under a mosquito net while drunk often proves somewhat of a tricky maneuver, so the perpetrators are often caught in the act. Even if they escape, they may be recognized in the gloom and later teased mercilessly. If caught in the act, they can expect a sound beating from the woman's male kin.

The second form of sexual coercion that *Butaritari* recognize is the *tautau* or "holding." Whereas *kawakawa* is thought of as a mischievous, boyish, and relatively harmless act, *tautau* is considered pathological and evil. This is where sexual coercion is maintained with the threat of physical pain, brutality, or death. The social construction of this form of sexual violence is well-exemplified in the following paraphrased version of an incident in 1978:

> *The woman was asleep in an open house with a friend and a young daughter, and her brother and another friend were sleeping nearby. Two men came and, grabbing the wife and holding a knife at her throat, asked where her husband was. When she told them her husband was out fishing, they told her she would "suffer the consequences" of hiding her husband, and they were going to have sex with her. One of the men cut the strings of the mosquito net over the younger brothers, so they were caught up in the net. The woman was then grabbed by the hair and dragged down a track beside the house by one of the men, while the other remained and held her family at knife-point. Down the track the first man, holding her at knife-point, raped her. When he fell asleep, the woman got up, threw the knife away, and ran to the nearby house of her sister, who alerted the police. At the trial the two men argued they had raped the woman because her husband had been sexually involved with their sister, and they were exacting revenge.*

Several key features of this case make it a classic *tautau* episode in the Butaritari typology of sexual violence. First, it involved a married woman, so the implication is that the woman could not have initiated the sexual encounter. Second, the rape was in the village, which is considered a public arena. This is another index that the woman was obviously not "looking for it" or "asking for it."

Of the four women I interviewed who had been coerced into sex by men they were not married to, all found themselves unable to interpret their experiences as *tautau* incidents because they did not conform to these prescriptions. In all cases the women were unmarried, and the incidents took place in the bush rather than the village. As a result they are unable to shift blame for the incident from themselves to their assailants. Rather, the community, friends, and family thought of the encounters as having "just got a little out of hand." In three of the four cases, the women were virgins. They were expected to passively accept their fate after the event, even though the loss of their virginity meant they were thereafter marked as *nikiranroro* and unable to make good marriages. They were denied the possibility of a socially legitimized retribution against their attackers.

Other ambiguities in local interpretations of what constitutes consensual sexual activity and what does not stem from the cultural maxim that it is improper behavior for young women to say "no" to any man who asks her a question. The idea of sex as a competition or "game," and the problem men have interpreting women's replies, is represented in the following comments by an older woman:

Some women use sex for games to make themselves proud. A girl will be proud and tell others if she meets a man and he only plays with her skin and doesn't have sex. If a man forces you to have sex, then he loses the game. He must be clever, and you must agree because he is clever. If he loses and has sex without you agreeing, then you will say he won only because of his strength instead of his knowledge. . . . For Butaritari girls "yes" always means "no," and "no" means "yes." In the south the girls are different. When they say "no," they mean "no." . . . Our girls are taught never to say "no," for this would be rude. You must never say "no" to even old men. You must only say "I will think about it."

Butaritari women are known for their fickle hearts and the love games they play with men—the so-called mouths of the north. To tease a young man, a young woman sometimes agrees to an evening meeting with a man, and then she will stand him up or spy on him from a distance with a group of her friends while he waits for her. To many young women, a man's declaration of love is a joke, a source of flattery. If a young man tells her he loves her, she may reply in agreement either for fun or because she is too shy to disagree with him. This in itself sometimes results in very different male and female interpretations of whether or not a sexual episode was consensual.

Some Comments on Violence in Butaritari   That women feel at risk of sexual violence is hardly a unique ethnographic situation. Some anthropologists have gone so far as to argue that the coercive constraint of female sexuality by threat or use of male violence is a human universal; that is, it appears in all human societies. Certainly, wife bashing and violence against women in general are so common cross-culturally, and so clearly correlated with status differentials between men and women, that recent anthropological treatments of the subject have pointed out that it is harder to explain why it is nearly absent or apparently absent in a few societies than why it is so common in others.

If Butaritari marriages can be violent, it may be unrealistic to expect that occasional violence—verbal or physical—is either extraordinary or even necessarily negative. Certainly, violence in Butaritari marriages can be seen to go in two directions, especially if verbal abuse—the Butaritari women's mode of expressing dissatisfaction, anger, and frustration—is interpreted as a balance to the more characteristically male mode of physical aggression. But Butaritari women make the clear distinction between an occasional cuffing and quarrelling in marriage and an unwarranted bashing, and it is men, they say, who always precipitate extreme, unbearable violence.

My interpretation of male violence in Butaritari also may rest on the harsh side. Certainly, before I lived on Butaritari, I had never been exposed to severe marital violence. The stories, sounds, and signs of violence initially stunned me and then made me very angry. The anger women expressed in interviews when they discussed violence was powerful and almost crushing. For many, it was the first time they had attempted to construct a narrative of some of the more difficult experiences of their lives, a unique opportunity to talk about things they felt deeply under relatively neutral conditions. The experience was often exhausting for us both. I now realize I took on much of the angry emotion expressed by women in interviews. I still am struggling to pull that anger out of my writing, and maybe I am not always successful.

Even further, in many cases the trust of the women, so fundamental to my research, was given with either explicit or implicit agreement that I would not only record their words but also present them in the way they wanted, in this case giving voice to what they see as their special pain. Another anthropologist's interpretation of Butaritari culture might be much more joyous and celebratory. The women of Butaritari embrace such positive passions often and with gusto, and their extraordinary humor and patience proved invaluable to my research and my Butaritari experience. But to the women whom I was working with, befriended, and developed a close relationship with, this joyousness was not the aspect of or perspective on their lives that they felt was most important to transmit to me and through me to others.

And, on a final note, some marriages are characterized by a pleasant lack of conflict; here are the words of one of those women, speaking of her husband:

We have never quarreled, ever. We just let each other do what we wish. This wasn't a decision; rather, it was always this way. I've never been koko *because I have nothing to be* koko *about. He is a good man, hard working, and very kind to me. We don't argue because if I get angry, he just makes me laugh.*

3 / Women's Reproductive Health

Nei Tibe and I arrive at the house, and Nei Nera* is stretched out on the platform. Nera has had back pains since her last birth and has requested Tibe's help to fix the problem. Tibe hangs herself off the edge off the platform and calls for a pot of cold water and a piece of cloth. She arranges Nera on her back, so she can lean onto her outstretched body. Dipping her hands in the water and shaking them behind her, she puts her thumb in Nera's navel. "Feel this," she says, and indicates I should place my thumb in the navel as she had. "Just as I thought," she continues, "the beat-beat of the kai *is not in its right place. You should be able to feel it strongly under your thumb. She fingers slowly clockwise around the stomach, then takes my hand and places it on a spot several inches from the navel. "This is the place," she says, "the beat-beat there shows where the* kai *has moved to." Tibe dips the cloth into the cool water and wads it into a tight ball, then begins rhythmically rolling it across Nera's stomach toward her navel. She explains, "It's the heat of the birth that made the* kai *wander. That's what gives Nera the pain. It is the cold that will make it go back to where it should be in the middle of the stomach." She turns Nera onto her side and begins a similar rolling across her back toward the center. Placing her on her back again, she puts her thumb back in Nera's navel. Obviously satisfied with the result, she motions me to feel again. "See," she says, "now the beat-beat is back in the middle where it should be. There will be no more pain." Then she chuckles, "Nei Nera, you might have no pain for now, but you will have to beware of your husband—now you might get pregnant. Maybe you want me to put it back—backache may be less trouble than being busy with another baby."*

I began collecting information on how Butaritari women perceive their reproductive anatomy by asking women to fill in a blank outline of a female form with the locations of reproductive organs and to explain how they worked. These interviews proved successful at getting women to talk about their bodies and also very popular—that is, except with virgins, who were unwilling or unable to articulate anything at all about the reproductive process. This is predictable, given that knowing the words for sexual organs in particular is tantamount to an admission of sexual experience—something at which a Butaritari virgin would not want to even hint.

Women—whether housewives or *nikiranroro*—presented varied models of their reproductive physiology and anatomy. Much of the information is passed during healing episodes, in which the healer explains how and why she is treating the patient. Because some healers obtain healing knowledge in dreams, the ideas women pick up from them during healing sessions can be varied. Certain themes emerge consistently about female reproductive health. The most pervasive are the importance of left-right alignment in the body and the dangerous role of heat. (Heat in the abdomen is seen as the root of most illness in the Kiribati healing system.)

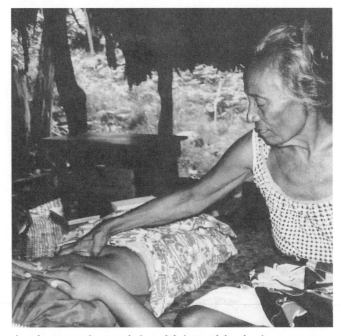

Nei Tibe at work with a patient, locating the beat of the kai *with her thumb.*

Two central organs are described in relation to women's reproduction: the cervix and the *kai*. The latter is an organ roughly analogous to what I think of as the uterus; that is, it is the place where a baby develops and where menstrual blood comes from. The *kai* has features that make it unlike a uterus as well: Men also are said to have a *kai*, which is smaller than women's and is the source of semen. The *kai* is visualized as an unanchored organ about fist size, which in a healthy woman sits directly below the navel. The other vital reproductive organ, the cervix, is described as a small round organ that is the "doorway" to the body. This doorway opens when women menstruate to let the blood out from the body, and women say the cervix is also the place where all vaginal mucus originates.

In the Butaritari model, these two central organs, the cervix and the *kai* (which I will call the uterus for simplicity's sake), are aligned in the center of the body. They are separate organs, and between them is a watery area (see Figure 7). This watery area is the region in which the uterus can wander. When the uterus wanders from its centrally aligned place under the navel, pain and infertility are the symptomatic outcome. If it goes upward into the chest, the woman will have nausea; if sideways, she may have backache or pain in her legs. Healers explain that this movement results from heavy lifting or falls or from any overheating in the abdomen, such as from a fever. To relocate a wandering uterus, healers choose light massage and cooling therapies to help return the organ to under the navel, just as Tibe did at the opening of this chapter.

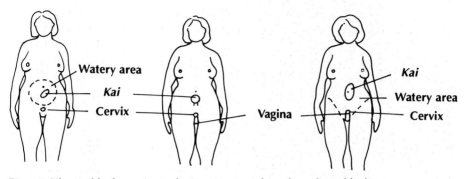

Figure 7 Three models of women's reproductive anatomy, as drawn by traditional healers.

GETTING PREGNANT

The Butaritari notion of how women get pregnant and how a baby forms flow from this anatomical model. Nei Rona*, a healer from Butaritari village, described this process so succinctly, it is better left to her words:

> *When you have sex, and you and your partner both orgasm at the same time, his thing knocks against the cervix, and it makes the cervix open. The door of the cervix opens when the woman orgasms. Then his semen can enter your body because now the way is open. When it enters it mixes with the woman's [procreative juice] in the watery area of the stomach we call the "high tide." When these two [male and female] juices meet, they mix together, and this is the start of a person. This mixture goes up to the uterus, and that is where it stays and grows. It feeds on the blood: That is why you don't have your period while you are pregnant, because the baby feeds on the blood. In the first three months, the baby is not properly human; it is like the lizard. Boys become like humans sooner than girls. At about three or four months, the boy will start to flutter in the woman's stomach. The girl starts to move at about five months. Then it will be like a human.*

INFERTILITY

The Butaritari model of how pregnancy occurs also explains why some women have trouble conceiving: The uterus or cervix may be out of alignment, so the semen cannot enter the body; the prehuman fluid mixture gets lost in the "high tide" of the abdomen; the woman is not orgasmic, so the cervix is not opening to let semen into her body; menstrual blood may not be "compact" in the uterus, so a baby cannot feed and dies; or abdominal heat may curdle and kill the woman's procreative juice.

When women start to suspect they are infertile—for example, if they have been married for more than eighteen months and have not become pregnant—they may seek the help of local healers or skilled family members. (Problems with lack of female orgasms are considered the husband's responsibility.) But even though the quest for motherhood has powerful underlying motivations related to a need to produce heirs to solidify a marriage and protect land inheritance, women are very casual in seeking ethnomedical help for infertility. This is because the option of adoption fills these needs for infertile couples. The words of Nei Tokaua* underscore the value placed on adoption as a response to childlessness, if only because her case shows the lengths to which a woman denied the adoption option might be willing to go. Neither Tokaua nor her husband are from the island. At the time she made the following statement, she had no relatives from whom to adopt, and she was in her early twenties and had been married three years. Tokaua had never visited a local healer to seek treatment for her childlessness.

> *We always planned a family, but I think there is some problem. Sometimes I have pain in my side, and my period doesn't always come with the moon. But there are no family for either of us to adopt from here. I have this secret plan, to have a child. Do you remember that* I Matang *couple who visited on the yacht a few weeks ago? She was really pregnant, and now they are on Tarawa waiting for the baby to be born. I think if I ask them for the child, they would want me to have it. But I haven't told [my husband] yet, as it is still a secret plan—I think he will be comfortable with the idea.*

I then asked: "Do you think there would be any problem with an *I Matang* child being raised by *I Kiribati?*"

> *Oh, no. There would be no problem. That child would be given things as my own child would. The* I Matang *[mother] would know that and would be pleased.*

"What if they say 'no' to the adoption?"

> *Then I might just have to take the child myself anyway. That would be better for the child because the child would have everything it wanted. In the end the parents would agree once it is my child and they see that. That is my secret plan.*

Luckily, Tokaua did not need to try and follow through with her plan. Several months later her husband's family on another island provided them with a young girl for adoption. Last time I saw her, she was happily leading her new daughter down to the shoreline, holding her hand tightly and with a proud smile lighting her face. It was the first time I had seen her looking genuinely happy in the months I had known her.

In fact, apparent sterility is a rare experience for Butaritari women. The proportion of married women who, like Tokaua, have never had a live birth is very low on Butaritari, less than 2 percent. Of the 110 women I interviewed who had been married and sexually active for more than ten years, only one had never given birth. This is one of the lowest marital infertility rates recorded for any human group and the lowest I have come across in the Pacific region. The first reason infertility is so rare in this population is that such sexually transmitted diseases as gonorrhea, syphilis, and genital chlamydia are essentially absent. Second, couples often remain married for years, even if they do not have any children early; women are not necessarily divorced just for being childless. Also, because couples are generally having lots of sex, they have plenty of chances to get pregnant. With adoption as a back-up, all these factors combine to create a social environment in which women have several possible paths to follow in their quest for motherhood.

WHAT IS UNHEALTHY, AND WHAT DO YOU DO ABOUT IT?

Butaritari women's ideas about reproductive health are intimately connected to their ideas about what is an attractive and appropriate sexuality for women. At an abstract level, the difference between men's and women's sexuality in Butaritari society is portrayed in a series of dual oppositions: strong-weak; aggressive-passive; wild-tame; public-private; reef-lagoon; left-right; male-female. Male sexuality is thought of as wilder, less predictable, and difficult to keep under rein. Female sexuality is passive, malleable, and less explosive.

More specifically, the two feminine qualities women equate with an attractive and healthy sexuality are reflected in the two insults women consider particularly offensive. First, to really insult a woman, you would say she is like a dog who "cannot look after herself," most cuttingly that she "stinks"—the Kiribati word implies a really distasteful genital smell. Second, it is considered ghastly to be a woman labeled as "wet like the ocean." Butaritari women believe men prefer to have sex with a woman if her vagina is dry, making it tighter. It is common practice among married women to clean out the vagina once or twice each day to remove all vaginal mucus, not only because the mucus is said to be itchy and unsexy, but also because it is thought to stink. For special occasions, some women make small packages of sweet-smelling leaves tied in mosquito netting to insert in the vagina to make their genitalia smell sweet.

One of the most extreme traditional medical procedures practiced in Kiribati is the *kotokoto,* a form of cervical cauterization designed to prevent vaginal mucous and to make the woman extremely sexy and sexually satisfying to men. As one woman noted:

> *This woman is ugly and lazy, and we never know why her husband doesn't leave her, because he is beautiful and hard working. But then we found out she had the* kotokoto, *so we understood. That is why her husband stays with her and never goes to other women, even though she has never had a child. He prefers the woman who has done the* kotokoto.

Although this is traditionally a practice particular to the more southern atolls of the chain, spates of *kotokoto* have occurred in Butaritari over the last few decades. The practice has fallen out of favor—in part because only a few women know how to conduct the *kotokoto* but mostly because of a strong—and real—perception among women that it is a life-threatening practice. Many stories circulating in the women's community tell of women who died after they used the *kotokoto.* As one woman warned me:

> *If you use the* kotokoto, *you will never live to be fifty-something years old. Every woman who does it dies at forty-something, even if they only do it just one time.*

In all, I came across five cases of women from Butaritari village who were rumored to have died from using the *kotokoto* in the last few decades. Three of the five were labeled *nikiranroro,* and these are the women said to use the practice most often. By doing the *kotokoto,* they are thought to increase their power of *tatanako*—that is, to make all men drawn to them, even against the men's will. Generally, married women only consider doing the *kotokoto* if they fear the reason their husband strays so often to other women is because he "notices the difference" and prefers a woman who is drier, tighter, and sweeter smelling.

For the *kotokoto,* direct heat application is used on the cervix or vaginal entrance to inhibit vaginal and cervical secretions. *Kotokoto* treatments involve heating a long, thin reef stone, which is about the size and shape of a middle finger, on embers until it is red hot. The hot stone is then touched to the cervix or the outer edges of the vagina. The woman has "watery secretions" for about one to three months after the treatment, after which time the secretions will stop altogether, and the process is complete. Women contend that it is extremely important not to have sex in the intervening period because to do so would cause the vagina to "go rotten" and disappear. The following account was given by a woman describing a friend who was said to have died from using the *kotokoto:*

> She was sick for a long time. There was always smelly water and blood coming out from her. In the end there was no vagina left, only a hole where it should be. That was because of the kotokoto. There was just nothing inside; you could see all the way inside to her intestines.

I had no opportunities to watch the procedure being done, mainly because it is done so rarely, but also because, I suspect, women are reluctant to admit they have practiced *kotokoto.* However, I do have the following account, related to me by a woman who had watched a specialist at work:

> Nei Oro* [from a southern atoll] got the woman to sit with her legs apart and up a little. Then she told her to push out like she was trying to shit. That was so the edges of the vagina would stand out. Nei Oro took a small basin and put it in front of the woman. Inside were dried fibrous pandanus-fruit centers that were burning with small stones on top to keep in the heat. She took the stone and heated the tip on the stones in the bowl. Then she touched the vagina with the tip, the part of the vagina you can see. It made a "ssss" sound when it touched. She touched all around the sides of the vagina to complete it.

From a biomedical perspective, such practices would inhibit vaginal and cervical secretions. The cauterization of the cervix would damage the mucous-producing glands, as well as possibly introducing infection and even making the woman sterile. The cauterization of the vaginal entrance would damage Batholin's glands, which provide sexual lubrication.

To keep the *kotokoto* in some perspective, I would argue it is something like a Butaritari version of breast augmentation—a Western practice that Butaritari women find puzzling and ridiculous, as the following extract from my journal shows:

> Nei Mareve and I sat around in the house after we had been to see a video in the *maneaba*. This week's choice was *Dolly Sings*. Mareve was fascinated by the size of Dolly Parton's breasts and began to explain to me why that was so unattractive to Kiribati men—how they got in the way and "interrupted things" between a man and a woman. She began questioning me about what *I Matang* men like, and I told her about how some *I Matang* women have their breasts enlarged just to make themselves more attractive to men. She sat there quietly for a minute thinking about this, with her eyebrows raised to show she thought it curious at the very least. With laughter in her voice, she replied, "I know: It must be that *I Matang* men really like to breastfeed, even though they aren't

babies anymore—that must be what they really want, never to be weaned." (Field Journal, January 31, 1991)

Another important symptom of good health to Butaritari women is regular menstruation. Women track their periods by cycles of the moon, marking the time each is due by the place of the moon in the sky. Menstruation is seen as healthy because it takes "old" blood out from the body. The single-most-feared reproductive complaint is a form of "retention sickness" called *te tibu,* where the uterus becomes filled with menstrual blood trapped in the body. If left untreated, this disease is thought to kill— the uterus will keep expanding until the woman dies. The ultimate cause of *tibu* is thought to be heating in the abdomen.

Women say it is unsafe to swim when they are menstruating, because the cervix is open at this time, and water will be able to seep into the body. If this happens, they warn, the insides can get waterlogged and go rotten.

(In many parts of the Pacific, menstrual blood is seen as a particularly dangerous and polluting fluid that can harm men. This notion of menstrual pollution is not as pronounced on Butaritari, and women are not secluded from men while they menstruate. Many couples resist sex during menstruation, though, considering that if the man comes into contact with the blood, he may get skin rashes or feel weak. However, some women mentioned the occasional bit of sex during menses would not do men much harm, and they said sometimes their husbands might initiate this when they had been drinking.)

Perhaps the most unusual reproductive condition women identify is the *buanuri* or eel, which several older woman claimed to have either had or seen. The *buanuri* begins as an "egg" attached to the vagina wall or in the cervix, about the size of a hen's egg. The egg may appear if the woman has been doing hard work too soon after a birth. It hatches into an eel, which makes its home in the vagina. According to one skilled healer:

> *There is a kind of sickness some women say they have like an eel that lives in the stomach. But it will come down if you sit beside the fire and cook fish and put your leg up while you are sitting. The eel will smell the fish and come out the vagina. If you take the fish and put it farther and farther away, you can tempt the eel out. But you must be careful, I think, because if you kill the eel, then you can kill the woman. There was a very old woman in another village who died that way. They cut the eel with a knife when it came out to get the fish, and she died. Everyone saw it come out.*

My guess is that, biomedically, the *buanuri* is a postpartum hernia.

A particularly dreaded reproductive condition is *te kiriti,* literally called "grease" because the uterine growth of the condition (the mole) looks like white animal grease when it is taken from the body. Of 210 women I interviewed in depth about their reproductive histories, three had experienced a *kiriti* pregnancy, and I also turned up several cases of women from Butaritari village who had reportedly died of the condition over the previous three decades.

From a biomedical perspective, *te kiriti* refers to gestational trophoblastic disease (GTD). This is a disease of the trophoblast, the ectodermal tissue that links the embryo to the uterus in pregnancy, formed by the embryo. GTD shows great variation in incidence in different human groups. Butaritari GTD rates, as much as I can ascertain from women's self-reports, are 4.27 per 1,000 noted pregnancies, an extremely high incidence and about four times the rate for the United States.

The symptoms of GTD begin as very similar to those of pregnancy—no periods, nausea and vomiting, and a swelling abdomen—but the symptoms are exaggerated; the stomach swells too fast, the nausea is extreme, and the woman is very fatigued. Sometimes a fetus is present, but the uterus becomes increasingly enlarged. In some cases the condition occurs only once and is benign. In others, it can develop into an aggressive, malignant tumor that kills the mother within weeks. Although a genetic basis to the disease is now established, the exact mechanism is unclear, and the role of environmental factors in risk for developing the disease or the form it takes is unclear, which makes it difficult to figure out exactly why the disease is so common on Butaritari. A factor seems to involve the male partner; the growth in the uterus is foreign to the woman's body and contains the partner's genetic material (as contributed by his sperm). It may be some form of immune response between the woman and her partner that triggers the condition.

To the Butaritari, heat in the abdomen is thought to be one possible cause of the disease. *Te kiriti,* according to local experts, is "not a real baby" because it is killed by the *kiriti* before it takes on human form. All healers agree the pregnancy must be terminated and the mole removed, or the woman would die. This is done through abdominal massage, or it may evacuate spontaneously. In some cases the clinic has arranged for women to be airlifted to Tarawa to have the tissue removed in the hospital.

HEALING AND HEALERS

The majority of women's health care is provided by local healers in the village, the clinic nurse, and the local midwives, who also often work at the local clinic. These "nurse-aides" have no biomedical training, and all much prefer to treat illness with herbal drinks, massage, and magic than with Western medicine. They are paid around $6 a week for this work. The government provides them with around $3 extra for each delivery they oversee, all of which currently take place in homes, rather than the clinic. This makes for an interesting mix of Western and Kiribati medicine being practiced at the clinic.

These women learn their skills from older, knowledgeable people who give them the information as part of an inheritance to a special family member or friend. (Sometimes men work as healers, although less commonly. Men tend to specialize in bone-setting, an art at which the Kiribati excel.) Almost all medicinal recipes are family secrets and are passed as special knowledge between close kin or friends with a special relationship to the expert. Some families have a tradition of healing knowledge, while other families do not. Recipes are also secret, in that it is demeaning to ask someone else for a recipe instead of being passed it as a gift. Luckily, people did not apply this principle to me, in the sense that women were very open in sharing recipe details with me. Giving the recipes to an outsider, especially one from another country, is not considered to be breaking any secrets within the community, and I promised not to use the "secrets" to practice on the island.

Most medicines are based on the juice of leaves and fruits of the limited number of plants that grow on the island, infused in or mixed with water. All recipes work on a principal of the number three or its multiples—for example, three leaves, three days, three times. Three is a special and magical number in Butaritari healing and magic arts. Here is one recipe that is typical in this regard:

> *If you are about four or five months pregnant and you think you might lose the baby, you can use the* kiaou *fruit* [Triumfetta procumbens]. *You take the unripe fruit and squeeze it into rainwater. The juice is very slippery and will make the baby slip out quickly. If you are bleeding and you use the fruit, the baby will either slip out quickly or the baby will live and the bleeding will stop. If the baby is to die, it will happen quicker. This will not hurt the woman. You use 150 fruit the first time, and give the treatment three times.*

Illness considered to have a natural—rather than supernatural—origin, such as any of the conditions thought to arise from abdominal heating, is treated with massage and herbal drinks. Although conversion to Christianity has curtailed any open use of magic, it remains an important component of the healing system in Butaritari. This is because the ultimate cause of many conditions—such as sterility or mental illness—is thought to be due to malicious magic, which can be countered only with magic. This is exemplified in a story told by Nei Retina* about her second pregnancy:

> *While I was pregnant, I started having these dreams about an* I Matang *man with curly hair. The dreams would come when I slept in both the night and the day, but when he would come at night, I would always feel sick the next morning. This started after I went on a visit to Keuea village. I went to shit on the east-side beach, but then people from Keuea told me there was a spirit living on that beach. The spirit must have followed me home when he saw me. I would dream he had sex with me, but it was all right because it didn't hurt the baby at all, I don't think. But it did mean I had a hard time eating while I was pregnant because I felt sick. After the baby was born, I started to have heavy bleeding. Nei Rona* came to see to the bleeding, and I told her about the* I Matang *spirit. She mixed some medicine and said some magical words. After that, the bleeding stopped, and the spirit left my dreams.*

Pregnant women are particularly careful about the risks of being exposed to the malicious mischief of spirits, who lurk in the dark, in the bush, and on beaches. When pregnant, especially before the fourth or fifth month, a woman needs to watch her movement to keep herself beyond their reach and should stay in the safer areas around her own household as much as possible. A woman may be unaware that she has been "caught" by a spirit until she later experiences something abnormal, such as pregnancy complications, a congenital defect, or a dream in which the spirit is featured. Not all magic is that of spirits, though; malicious intent by humans is thought to be the cause of some illness. If a couple has no children, a suspicion might develop that another relative wanting to inherit their landholdings is practicing magic to make the woman sterile.

The models women invoke to describe their own reproductive systems have a substantial impact on whether women choose to use contraceptives and how they use them if they do, and this has been observed by anthropologists under a wide variety of cultural settings. In Butaritari, how women think contraceptives work, especially in their role in "heating" the body, has made two of the most reliable methods—injectable contraceptives and The Pill—unpopular as birth-control methods.

Women never use any method of contraception between marriage and their first birth. However, some use a traditional or biomedical method to space or stop births once they have at least one living, healthy child. When I did my first surveys, eighty-two women in my sample were sexually active and not pregnant (as assessed by a pregnancy test or recent period), meaning they were potentially susceptible to becoming pregnant. Of these, 18 percent were practicing some form of pregnancy avoidance—with a clinic contraceptive, a traditional method, or by periodic abstinence or celibacy. Of these, only one half were opting for (more reliable) clinic methods (The Pill, the IUD, the injectable). Given the government efforts to lower fertility on Butaritari and the aggressive family-planning program behind that effort, this is a very low use rate. The reasons acceptance is so low relate to a broad and complex series of issues, including fear of side effects and a strongly pro-natalist social milieu. Nei Abo's account shows how the decision making part of the equation is anything but simple, is more than economic, and is very difficult to trace:

> Nei Abo* [a *nikiranroro*] arrived this morning while I was doing laundry and stood just around the edge of the house, hiding from everyone's line of vision but mine, then motioned me back to her house with some seeming sense of urgency. When I got there, she sat me on the platform and, reaching up into the roof thatch, pulled out a blister-pack of oral contraceptives. I started asking her why she had got them, and she explained she had a new boyfriend and couldn't afford any more children by herself. It appears Abo got the pills quietly from one of the nurse-aides at the clinic last week, but the nurse-aide had been unable to explain to her how she should use them, I guess because she simply hadn't known. Abo said she was unsure if she should take them all at once or not and was too shy to ask anyone else because she didn't want people to know about her new boyfriend [I assume he's someone's husband]. She asked me to show her how to take them, and I very carefully went through the procedure—when she should start and what to do if she missed one and so on. She made me go through it several times, and I then I wrote it on a scrap of paper for her, and she seemed very confident and happy by the time I left—and she put the paper and the pills carefully back into the thatch. (Field Journal, March 13, 1991)

Shortly after, Nei Abo was pregnant. She was highly motivated to stop herself from becoming pregnant. She was already feeling the stress of two children and, without a regular partner and with her family on another island, she has little practical or emotional support. She has no land on Butaritari and is struggling to run a small store to make ends meet. But, even with the means and information at her disposal that she had sought out to control her fertility, she became pregnant within weeks and later gave birth to another daughter. Her new daughter, she says now, brings her enormous joy and will care for her in her old age.

This does not mean women do not wish to avoid pregnancy. Of these identified women susceptible to pregnancy, almost three-quarters said they did not want to get pregnant then, yet they were not practicing any form of birth control and were sexually active. This gap between a stated desire to limit family size and a lack of any attempt to prevent pregnancy has been noted, frustratingly, by the government. The two explanations most often offered are "religious resistance" and what is euphemistically called "partner factors" (that is, uncooperative husbands). With regard to "difficult" husbands, women stated this was not the case—their husbands were very supportive of wishes to limit their family size; in fact, 93.1 percent stated so. And religious resistance is not an adequate explanation either: No real difference occurs between Catholic and non-Catholic fertility on the island.

Only a quarter of all Butaritari women have ever tried to use a clinic contraceptive method (see Figure 8 for which methods). And, as Nei Abo's story shows, even when clinic methods are used, method failure can occur because of inconsistent use and high "drop-out" rates. The reasons women give for not continuing these methods focus substantively on their side effects, and these link directly to the way women see their reproductive anatomy and interpret symptomology of their reproductive health.

Women are unsure how oral contraceptives affect fertility, although some think the pill may kill the female procreative fluid by heating the abdominal region. This dangerous heating effect on the body could therefore cause an enormous array of diseases. Breastfeeding women are particularly cautious of using The Pill, concerned that the heating effect will taint breast milk and make the child ill with diarrhea and vomiting. One advantage women note of The Pill is that their periods are regular when they use it—this being an index of good health. One other mentioned side effect of The Pill is an increase in feelings of vaginal wetness or mucous production and an increase in unpleasant vaginal odor, which are considered by women as particularly sexually undesirable.

When the Lippes loop intrauterine device (IUD) was first introduced in the Butaritari clinic in the late 1960s, women were extremely enthusiastic about the new method. As one woman put it: "We couldn't believe what they said—we all actually jumped up and *ran* to the clinic." At present, however, the "loop" is considered a dangerous and unpleasant contraceptive option. One fear associated with the loop is the story, which has now circulated through village gossip for several years, of a woman who died after a loop "traveled into her stomach" and killed her.

The loop, Butaritari women say, sits in or on top of the cervix. It works by killing either the man's or the woman's procreative juice. Because the area above

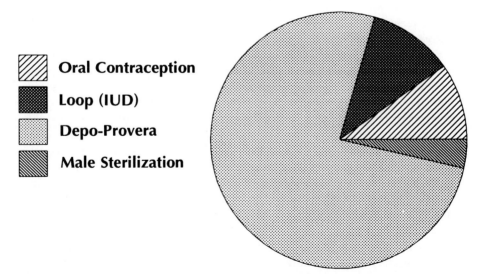

Figure 8 Clinic-based contraceptive methods in use in Butaritari village in mid-1990. All eighty-three women represented in this graph are married, with at least one living child.

where the loop sits is empty of all organs and filled with liquid, it is possibile the loop can become unattached, travel freely upward, and damage internal organs. If a woman becomes pregnant while using a loop, it is thought to be potentially damaging to the fetus, causing congenital deformations such as harelip and cleft palate or birthmarks. (Harelip and cleft palate are heritable conditions. Seven people have harelip in Butaritari village, whom a bit of genealogical detective work showed all shared a common ancestor three generations ago.)

Depo-Provera injectable is the most popular clinic contraceptive method used on Butaritari at present, in part because it is the method most aggressively promoted by clinic staff. (Depo-Provera has been a widely used contraceptive in many parts of the world for several decades. It was only recently approved for release in the United States by the Food and Drug Administration.) The most often cited problem with this method is the possibility of *te tibu* occurring, because menstrual blood is thought to be not released regularly. Women say the possibility of *te tibu* is much higher with Depo-Provera than with the loop because weight increases are noted by women using this method. It is the weight gain, rather than the cessation or irregularity of menstruation, that is the greatest concern. This is because the weight gain is considered a clear indicator that *te tibu* is in progress, as the uterus becomes full and heavy with "retained" menstrual blood. Because *te tibu* is thought of as a potentially fatal condition, women who perceive body changes indicative of *te tibu* are strongly motivated to stop using this method.

TRADITIONAL BIRTH-LIMITING METHODS

Several nonclinic or more traditional methods are in occasional use as birth control. Several healers in the village, like Tibe, have used manipulation of the uterus and the cervix as a means to prevent pregnancy, although all used it rarely. Pressing the side of the cervix with her index finger, the healer pushes the cervix downward and sideways. Among other things, one healer explained, this will stop the woman from having orgasms and will therefore stop pregnancy. This method is, unsurprisingly, not particularly popular, because it is known also to be both painful and not especially reliable. To manipulate the uterus, the healer uses massage on the abdomen. Once the uterus is "bent" in this way, the pre-fetus will not be able to "find its home"—an almost reverse pattern of the massage used to return a misplaced uterus to the center of the abdomen.

It is difficult to assess if this method is at all successful at preventing pregnancies, because I could not collect enough cases of women using it. But the three women who had used the method over several years assured me they were happy with it as a method for spacing out births, and in their minds it was successful at doing this. In fact, the "bent" uterus may be a form of retroversion, in biomedical terms. A retroverted uterus reduces the risk of pregnancy because the cervix is not fully covered by semen after sex.

Abortion is another birth-control option for some Butaritari women. Deliberate abortion has been limited mainly to *nikiranroro* pregnancies. Even among *nikiranroro*, though, few women personally consider abortion an alternative to having a child they did not plan. With an extensive adoption network, such value placed on motherhood, and the attention lavished on small babies, as well as a fatalistic view about such things once the woman is pregnant ("it's too late now"), unmarried women are only rarely forced into a situation where abortion becomes a real option. Some women have very strong anti-abortion sentiments. As one woman said, "People will say if she died that it was better anyway because she was trying to kill her baby."

It also must be kept in mind that the Butaritari are very fatalistic in perspective: Once they get over the surprise of an unplanned pregnancy, they generally resign themselves quickly and get on with preparing for motherhood. In regard to contraceptive and health-seeking behavior in Butaritari women, the role of this sense of fatalism toward both life and death cannot be understated. More often than not, they have a strong sense of what will be will be.

During the reproductive-history interviews I had, two women disclosed to me that they had induced abortions, and I suspect at least one other case. It seems induced abortion has become less common over the past century for several reasons. First, the influence of the Catholic Church has provided a "moral" discouragement of the practice. Second, women who are unmarried and pregnant are "ashamed" to seek the information from women outside the immediate kin circle, and medical knowledge is distributed unevenly among families. Therefore, some women have no opportunity for abortion because the necessary technical knowledge is not available to them. This does not, however, prevent attempts by the really intent, even if they do not "know the secret":

> When I had my last pregnancy, I was not married. I didn't tell my family I was pregnant because I was so ashamed and kept quiet. I didn't want a husband, and I wanted to play. I had no one to ask for help because I was shy and didn't know who to ask. I lay on my stomach on the edge of the house platform and rubbed my stomach up and down on the edge. I did this each day for about one week when I would first wake in the morning. Then the pain came, and the baby came.

Skilled women use less drastic methods, including drinks made from bitter plant leaves and roots in seawater. Each recipe generally includes only one or two plants, most often the leaves of the salt bush *(Scaevola sericea),* which lines the leeward side of the island, or the umbrella tree *(Messerschmidia argentea)*—both of which are common in the region and were likely on the island before it was first settled by humans. To my knowledge no one has made any pharmacological studies of these plants, so any abortifacient qualities have not been tested.

Massage techniques of abortion are also used; they are basically an inverse to massage used to retain and stabilize a fetus during pregnancy (that is, the direction of massage is reversed) and are much more vigorous. In many ethnomedical settings, massage is established as an effective means to bring on abortion. Often herbal drinks and massage are used in combination, the drinks being taken to "loosen" the baby and to prevent *post abortum* hemorrhage and the massage used to release the fetus. One woman also told me of a more unusual method: She places a half coconut shell with a hole over fire and squats over the shell with her vagina in direct line of the heat.

Despite healers claiming these methods are very successful as a means to abortion—of which I have no doubt—complications often follow. Hospital staff on Tarawa tell me septic abortion is a common outcome of these methods, and they see several cases each year. Regarding the two specific cases of induced abortion I was able to discuss directly and at length with the women involved, both women had been subsequently infertile, and one had ended up in the hospital about six weeks later for "a stomach operation," which was presumably linked to complications following the self-induced (unskilled) abortion.

SEXUAL BEHAVIOR AND DISEASE RISK

One interesting, and timely, example of how women's health, health behavior, and sexuality fit together in ecological or biocultural models is the behavioral dimension of the Butaritari population for contracting sexually transmitted diseases (STDs). Globally, STDs have been on the increase in the past decade. Older diseases, such as gonorrhea and syphilis, are burgeoning in many parts of the world, including parts of the Pacific, and syphilis has developed hardier, antibiotic-resistant strains. "New" diseases also have been appearing, such as HIV/AIDS.

Kiribati also has seen an increase in sexually transmitted disease cases in the past decade. Although the number of cases is still relatively low, the incidence of gonorrhea has increased substantially in the past decade (see Table 3-1). Few of these cases are on the outer islands, including Butaritari, however. Almost all are localized to the urban center of Betio islet, where nightclub culture is more developed and casual sexual contact is much more common. Kiribati has no sex-worker industry. As yet no infections with genital chlamydia, herpes, chancroid (soft chancre) or genital warts has been detected in Kiribati.

HIV, the virus that causes AIDS, has been identified in many of the nations of the Pacific. Kiribati is not exempt, and the first case of full-blown AIDS was discovered in the tuberculosis ward of Tungaru Central Hospital the week I completed fieldwork in July 1991.

The Kiribati government has been quick to accept the challenge of preventing the spread of HIV/AIDS in Kiribati and has launched campaigns to educate that—at least at the time of my stay—included a clear emphasis on promoting "a return to Christian morality." The main way information about HIV/AIDS is communicated to the broader public is through radio broadcasts. When I tried to get married women to discuss the ramifications of the disease in Kiribati—a topic they found particularly pointless and dull—they made it clear it could not be a disease of housewives, only *nikiranroro*. It is described as an *I Matang* disease, best avoided by not having sex with foreigners.

So, how great is the risk of HIV/AIDS becoming established in Kiribati? An ecological approach, which begins by integrating biological and sociocultural perspectives on sexual behavior, is one way to address such a question. Everything indicates that sexual transmission will be the main way the AIDS virus will be transmitted in Kiribati. The virus is spread through contact with body fluids, especially blood and semen. This is the same means as hepatitis B, a disease almost

TABLE 3-1   DISTRIBUTION AND INCIDENCE OF GONORRHEA CASES IDENTIFIED
IN GOVERNMENT CLINICS IN KIRIBATI IN 1990

	Urban (South Tarawa)		Rural (Outer Islands)	Total
	Excluding Betio	*Betio Only*		
Number of Cases	45 (28.5%)	74 (46.8%)	39 (24.7%)	158
Population Age 18 to 49 Years Only				
Population Age 18–49	7,240 (25.0%)	4,477 (15.4%)	17,278 (59.6%)	28,995
Incidence per 1,000	3.8	16.5	2.3	5.5
Total Population				
Total Population	15,928 (23.6%)	9,226 (13.7%)	42,319 (62.7%)	67,471
Incidence per 1,000	2.8	8.0	0.9	2.3

Distribution and incidence of gonorrhea cases identified in government clinics in the Tungaru/Gilbert chain in Kiribati, 1990. Cases are heavily concentrated in the area of Betio islet on the administrative and relatively urban capital of South Tarawa. Betio is the location of nightlife and nightclub activity on Tarawa. The incidence of the disease has increased tenfold between 1978 and 1990, and recent informal reports have indicated the start of an epidemic on Betio.

everyone on Butaritari has at some stage in their lives. However, the transmission of hepatitis B in Kiribati follows a specific pattern, in which small children infect each other as they play and live together, most likely through contact with the oozing ulcers that are part of a tropical childhood. As such, tracing the extent of hepatitis B infection does not provide much insight to a disease that relies on sexual activity for its transmission. AIDS will be more dependent on sexual contact because donor blood in Kiribati is screened, and clean-needle use in clinics has been aggressively and successfully promoted, both of which reduce the chances of transmission by nonsexual means. Further, male-to-male sexual contact is rare in Kiribati. Male-to-male sexual expression is not tolerated, and male homosexual roles are not socially accepted. The male social transsexuality expressed in the *binabinaaine* role, which I discussed in Chapter 2, is not only rare but also generally takes place within long-term, established relationships, if it ever has a sexual component. This means women will be as much at risk of getting the disease as men, and the main arena in which sexual transmission will take place is in heterosexual relationships. This has been called a "Type II pattern" by the World Health Organization and is the form that now characterizes the heavily HIV-infected regions of sub-Saharan Africa.

Risky Behavior

The risk of getting an STD depends on, first, who you have sex with and, second, what you do when you have sex. In regard to the latter, for example, anal intercourse tends to be riskier than vaginal intercourse because the virus finds the rectal membrane easier to cross; also, the membrane is often more torn or irritated in sexual activity. Although, of course, almost impossible to verify, Butaritari women are adamant that heterosexual couples do not have anal intercourse. Those hospital staff

I spoke with informally said they had not seen any signs of anal intercourse (such as anal forms of sexually transmitted disease) in any patients during many years of observation and examination. For women, having sex at times when the vagina is irritated or damaged increases the risk of acquiring the AIDS virus.

The practice of using vaginal inserts to promote dry and sweet-smelling genitalia, considered by women to be sexually pleasing to men, is a potentially risky behavior. Some evidence indicates that the use of intravaginal irritants by women in Zaire, also designed to dry and tighten the vagina as a means of heightening male sexual pleasure, can cause vaginal inflammation, erode vaginal mucosa, and place women at increased risk for contracting HIV (De Bruyn 1992).

All married women on Butaritari manually evacuate the vagina of all mucous daily and also habitually after intercourse. At times this may prove irritating to the vaginal entrance and walls, thereby increasing the risk of HIV acquisition. Women are at risk who engage in sex at a time when the vagina is lacerated or otherwise susceptible during the risky (but rare) practice of *kotokoto,* vaginal and cervical cauterization, designed to dry the genitalia and vagina to enhance male sexual pleasure during intercourse. Butaritari women are also having sex very soon after they have given birth, in some cases in response to a perceived risk to the breastfeeding child if they delay becoming sexually active until longer after the birth. This potentially risky sexual activity may occur when women have vaginal damage.

The potential for the spread of diseases that depend mainly on sexual contact for their transmission is influenced by the patterns of "sexual networking" within communities. By sexual networking, I mean the number and identities of the sexual partners with whom individuals come into sexual contact. The form of the network determines both the risk of each person getting the disease as well as the speed at which the disease infiltrates a community.

On Butaritari, the lack of social sanctions against male adultery, coupled with the limited availability of *nikiranroro* as extramarital sexual partners, constitutes the main network through which sexually transmitted disease can pass. Approximately half of all interviewed women married for more than five years said their husbands had had at least one extramarital affair in the previous five years.

With the *nikiranroro* being finite in number, and far fewer than the number of married men in each village seeking extramarital sex, these affairs are often short in duration, with the *nikiranroro* moving on to a new partner when someone more interested or interesting comes along. Men are most likely to seek the favors of *nikiranroro* when they drink, and the heaviest drinkers in the village tended to be those who most often seek, although not necessarily secure, the favors of *nikiranroro.*

Men who leave Kiribati for temporary out-of-country employment—especially the two thousand or so *I Kiribati* who serve as seamen on foreign vessels—are likely candidates for repeated introduction of HIV infection to the Kiribati population. These seamen tend to be absent for several months at a time, returning home by air during leave and the conclusion of contracts. Both married and single men may serve on foreign ships, the main lure being the cash income that can be sent home as remittances to wives and family. The collection of qualitative data on the sexual experiences and perceptions of this group of men, presumably by a male researcher, is of particular importance to more comprehensively predicting HIV-infection risk within the Kiribati population. In terms of my study, this is one obviously vital area of investigation that was essentially closed because of my gender. It is very difficult to ascertain the level of risky sexual contact these men have while they rest and recreate in foreign ports, although several wives reported husbands claimed premarital experience with foreign prostitutes. Medical care while working on these foreign vessels, mostly German lines, is said to be of a high standard and apparently effective at treating such STDs as syphilis. Unfortunately, the Kiribati hospital service keeps no records of STD infections acquired by off-island workers while they are away.

Certainly, the sexual networks exist to provide avenues for both the introduction of and spread of HIV infection in Butaritari communities. The dynamics of sexual activity outside marriage, centered among the finite number of *nikiranroro* in each village, makes it the prime focal point where sexually transmitted disease could be passed among married men and subsequently to their (faithful) wives. So, the mechanisms exist for the dispersal of sexually transmitted disease throughout the village to more than half of all couples, couples whose male partner has extramarital sexual liaisons. On the other hand, very little premarital sexual activity occurs on Butaritari, and this reduces the size and extent of sexual networks.

The same basic factor that protected Kiribati, and Butaritari, from a massive onslaught of sexually transmitted disease historically is still in effect. The very geographic location of the islands, away from popular tourist spots, and the lack of commercially exploitable resources have created a situation of relative isolation. The sexual networks reflect this relative isolation, with almost all sexual contact taking place among long-term community members. *Nikiranroro,* for example, rarely have sex with *I Matang.* This is not necessarily because they find the idea unattractive but, rather, because on Butaritari, at least, they do not meet many. It also bears mention that in many parts of Africa the desperate quest for motherhood has put more women at risk of HIV infection. There childless women are socially and emotionally disadvantaged; they may be divorced for childlessness and move through sexual partners more rapidly in their search for a pregnancy. In Kiribati, where married women can use adoption as a resolution for childlessness and as a means to deal with the problems of land inheritance—so central to the economic and social relations of the Butaritari—they are protected from having to seek biological maternity by such risky means.

4 / An Ecology
of Human Behavior

Many examples are woven into this text of the subtle and complex dynamics among human culture, biology, and behavior: the management of maternal health; sexual behavior across the life span; women's work of birth and lactation; the experience of infertile women and of mothers; patterns of contraception; and sexually transmitted diseases and sexual behavior developed in the last chapter. All these phenomena represent a lifetime of personal experience and biological transition for Butaritari women—puberty, marriage, sex, birth—knotted together into the fabric of Butaritari social relations that emphasizes the reproduction of the family as an important social theme. It is undesirable, if not impossible, to exactly delineate the separate roles of culture and biology as they define human behavior and experience, and the intersections become particularly important when placed in ecological perspective. These articulations are particularly apparent, and poignant, for Butaritari women, given the stark theater in which they live: small and finite land area, vast ocean, poor soils, few plant and animal species, and limited fresh water.

However marginal, the environment does not simply pose a limit that can be absolutely demarcated, defined, and responded to by human groups. No aspect of the environment exactly and directly determines human behavior or social structures, and environmental constraints do not automatically or directly cause cultural patterns. Rather, the environment provides part of the *context* that shapes culture and shapes appropriate responses to the challenges faced by human groups.

Following the example of STD risk in relation to historic, social, and ecological context, the relative isolation of the island—far from popular tourist spots and having few economic resources of interest to outsiders—has kept sexual networks insular as well, greatly reducing the flow of sexually transmitted diseases into the community. Inside the community, further risk of transmission is minimized by the operation of a sexual system that provides positive reinforcement for women to avoid premarital sex and negative sanctions against extramarital sex. As a result, historically relatively minor outbreaks of infections with STDs have occurred on the island, resulting in no widespread infertility through the period since European contact. This combines with a population history that has demonstrated resistance to collapse despite some dramatic shifts in political structure and religion and exposure to a whole string of new, infectious, and often lethal diseases by either remaining static or showing growth.

For those few women infected with sexually transmitted diseases, the risk of infertility follows. For women, failure to bear children within marriage can be both a personal grief and a social liability, given the value placed on the mothering role and

Two young girls play in the water in Ukiangang village.

the pity toward infertile women. On Butaritari the systems of land inheritance provide a workable solution for women denied bearing their own children; women who adopt out their children to childless couples are profiting their children by making them sole inheritors to the barren couple's lands, and the adoptive parents benefit by being bestowed with the opportunity for social parenting, thus cementing their fully adult status within the community and firming their marriage relationship both personally and socially.

The process in which workable solutions are applied to the problems posed by our broader environment is termed *adaptation*. Humans are unique among all species for their ability to rely on cultural answers to environmental puzzles. The ability of individuals or groups of people to respond appropriately to changes in the environment defines our adaptive capacity. This capacity to respond is a product of the union of our biological and cultural repertoires. Human adaptations need not be perfect solutions to the challenges of our environment; in fact, they rarely are. As is the case with the Butaritari sexual system reducing transmission of STDs through the community, and the obvious health advantage this confers, adaptation rests on a behavioral repertoire that is the result of historical contingency, rather than the product of a social system designed to address this particular problem. To be adaptations, biobehavioral and cultural responses just have to create or maintain compromises that are marginally successful.

Measures of health are one possible index by which our fit as individuals, populations, and sections of societies to the environments in which we live and create can be assessed. In communities where women have a relatively low social status and little access to wealth, and where their labor is considered far less valuable than that of men, less social investment is made in them, and women or girls will be sicker and have shorter lives than their male counterparts (MacCormack 1988). This is despite, all things being otherwise relatively equal, biologically speaking we expect women to outlive men by a number of years on average, as is the case in the United States today (Holden 1987). Butaritari women are not disadvantaged in the health stakes compared to Butaritari men, outliving them by five years on average. This is a demographic outcome of social statements about the relative value of the genders, showing a lack of any clear disparity. The social value placed on women, as mothers, as workers, and as inheritors of land, shows in this relative longevity. Women have good access to available health care, whether at the clinic or with traditional healers, and often are the gender that controls special healing knowledge. Although men are fed the prize parts of all meals first, women are nourished as well as possible, given the plant and animal species available on the atoll and the volume of food available to each household. Women's workload is not more physically taxing than that of men, although their working day can be longer: Butaritari on the whole enjoy an easy workday for a subsistent group. Women live in a social milieu that allows them to reduce their workload at times when they are seen as or feel vulnerable—at menarche, in pregnancy and after birth, and when growing older. Entry to motherhood, for example, is a positive, strong family- and community-supported experience for Butaritari women. They are fed well, sleep long, and are treated with special kindness and concern. This has implications for women's health: Pregnancy and birth are times when women feel clearly socially involved and supported, and their descriptions of their experiences speak of these transitions as times of feeling vital.

Another demographic or health index of the social value of women is how old baby girls are when they are weaned as compared to baby boys. In societies that place significantly more value on male children, boys are generally breastfed more often and for longer, and this is of a distinct advantage to their health and survival. On Butaritari no differential in age when male and female children are weaned occurs, and this feeds into the demographic outcome of baby girls having no greater risk of illness or dying than baby boys.

Health may be one of the clearer examples of the biology-culture dynamic, but another developed throughout this text is that of sexuality and sexual behavior on Butaritari. The ethnography of sexual behavior on Butaritari describes a society where both adult men and women enjoy sex, participating in sex with spouses often and with increasing age. Sex is a common activity within marriages, and the social currents of sexual jealousy between spouses maintain an environment that encourages couples to remain sexually active through their twenties and thirties and beyond. The demographic impacts of this are apparent: Women not using contraceptive methods continue having children through their thirties, a pattern that is unusual in nonindustrial human populations.

The maintenance of later-life fertility need not translate into high population growth rates. Women have a repertoire of devices for managing pregnancy, including a pluralistic range of traditional and biomedical antifertility methods. Despite the efforts of government agencies to encourage smaller family sizes, women often choose to have large families and not to use contraceptives, or to use them in ways that make them less effective. While the government sees the advantage of smaller families, a stable population size for promoting women's health and for sustaining land availability and resources, women see nonuse of contraceptives in almost the inverse sense. Inasmuch as many antifertility options are seen as unhealthy by women, large families are valuable for the social relations they engender and maintain, as a means to garner land resources for the family.

A biobehavioral complex that allows women to have as many children the second half of their reproductive spans as the first and that provides family-limiting options for women is potentially advantageous in the island setting by permitting a flexibility in fertility strategies that can respond to potential overpopulation, on the one hand, and on the other can address the risk of extinction faced by small populations that shrink below a viable size in the events of disasters—new disease, typhoons, drought, and so on.

Teitu, who was introduced in Chapter 2 on the eve of her wedding, brings this more theoretical perspective back to the experience of the individual woman. Although the event in which she participated, a virginity test, was a significant, personal experience for her, it was caught up in a complex behavioral and ecological web imbedded with the social concerns of reproduction of the family and access to land.

To Teitu, the loss of her virginity, if a little scary, signals a happy and proud time for her. Her marriage is accepted, and her status increases as a result. Her family proudly celebrates her virginity and marriage with gifts, songs, and dance. Teitu's wedding night is in the domain of human experience where aspects of our biology and culture intersect and are bridged in an apparent way. Not only is the loss of Teitu's virginity a biological event imbued with enormous social significance, but also it is a socially significant event with biological implications. It is Teitu's first exposure to the chance of becoming pregnant and, depending on Bakoa's sexual activity before he married, her first possible exposure to sexually transmitted disease. And, had the biology been different—had Teitu not bled on her wedding night—her life might have taken a sharp turn for the worse.

Within an environmental matrix, Teitu's marriage resulted from complex decisions made by her family, following their perceptions of economic need and advantage and wanting to benefit their daughter and her children. The concern expressed by her husband's family over her virginity links to concern over the legitimacy of her children as future inheritors of the lands of their father's family; if Teitu's sexual fidelity can be trusted, the paternity of her children is socially guaranteed, and her children have legitimate rights to her husband's lands. The virginity test is the socially recognized index of her potential fidelity to her husband and to her worth as a wife.

To the people of Butaritari, land is *everything*. The desire to extend the family's control over land permeates the social management and negotiation of Teitu's marriage, virginity, sexuality, and future motherhood. In this way, the real and perceived ecology of the atoll shapes Teitu's life and that of all the women of Butaritari.

Glossary of Kiribati Terms

ainenuma: housewife
anti: spirits
ataeinaine: young girl
babai: giant swamp taro
binabinaaine: men assuming the dress and personality of women
binabinamane: women assuming the dress and personality of men
buanuri: eel that inhabits the vagina
bubuti: irrefusable request
buto: small, sharp women's weapon
eiriki: courtesy sexual relationship between a woman and her husband's classifactory brother
I Kiribati: people of Kiribati
I Matang: foreigners, usually Anglo
kabubu: preserved food made from pandanus fruit
kai: primary reproductive organ (uterus in women)
kainga: communally held land, residence site of major kin group
kameaka: very promiscuous person, nymphomaniac, one who behaves "like a dog"
kanobutika: dancing and sexual play between members of the bride's and groom's families in celebration of a wedding
kawakawa: stealthy sexual violation (literally "creeping, crawling")
kiaou: creeping plant used in medicine
kiriti: (literally "grease"), an ill-formed pregnancy (hydatidiform mole pregnancy)
koko: conjugal sexual jealousy
kotokoto: touching with heat, cervical cauterization
mama: ashamed, embarrassed, shy, humiliated
maneaba: communal meeting house
nei: article or title preceeding female names
nikiranroro: unmarried nonvirgin (literally "remnant of the generation")
tatanako: sexual power, irresistibility
tautau: violent sexual coercion (literally "holding")
teinaine: female virgin
tibu: swollen, swelling
tinaba: cross-generational courtesy sexual relationship
uea: high chief, king
unaine: elderly, senior woman
unimane: elderly, senior man
uri: fragrant, white-flowered tree used medicinally
utu: generic term for family

Recommended Reading

Grimble, A. 1988. *Tungaru Traditions: Writings on the Atoll Culture of the Gilbert Islands.* Edited by H. E. Maude. Honolulu: University of Hawai'i Press.

Hereniko, V., and T. Teaiwa. 1993. *Last Virgin in Paradise.* Suva, Fiji: Mana Publications.

MacDonald, B. 1982. *Cinderellas of the Empire: Towards a History of Kiribati and Tuvalu.* Canberra: Australian National University Press.

Works Cited

Brown, J. 1992. Introduction: Definitions, assumptions, themes, and issues. In D. Counts, J. Brown and J. Campbell (eds.), *Sanctions and Sanctuaries: Cultural Perspectives on the Beating of Wives.* Boulder: Westview, 1–19.

Caplan, P. 1993. Introduction 2: The volume. In D. Bell, P. Caplan and W. J. Karim (eds.), *Gendered Fields: Women, Men and Ethnography.* New York: Routledge, 19–27.

De Bruyn, M. 1992. Women and AIDS in developing countries. *Social Science and Medicine* 34:249–62.

Holden, C. 1987. Why do women live longer than men? *Science* 238:158–60.

Irwin, G. 1992. *The Prehistoric Exploration and Colonization of the Pacific.* Cambridge: Cambridge University Press.

Lambert, S. 1941. *A Doctor in Paradise.* Melbourne: Specialty Press.

Leavitt, S. 1991. Sexual ideology and experience in a Papua New Guinea society. *Social Science and Medicine* 33:897–907.

MacCormack, C. 1988. Health and the social power of women. *Social Science and Medicine* 26:677–83.

Ortner, S. and H. Whitehead. 1981. Introduction: Accounting for sexual meanings. In S. Ortner and H. Whitehead (eds.), *Sexual Meanings: The Cultural Construction of Gender and Sexuality.* Cambridge: Cambridge University Press.

Pellow, D. 1980. Sexuality in Africa. *Trends in History* 4:71–96.

Stevenson, R.L.S. 1987, orig. 1896. *In the South Seas.* London: Hogarth.

Tuzin, D. 1991. Sex, culture and the anthropologist. *Social Science and Medicine* 8:867–74.

Wade, P. 1993. Sexuality and masculinity in fieldwork among Colombian blacks. In D. Bell, P. Caplan and W. J. Karim (eds.), *Gendered Fields: Women, Men and Ethnography.* New York: Routledge, 199–214.

Warren, C. 1988. *Gender Issues in Field Research.* Beverly Hills, CA: Sage.

Wilkes, C. 1856. *Narrative of the U.S. Exploring Expedition During the Years 1832–1842.* Philadelphia: Lea and Blanchard.

Index